To

Candy

From

Love Harriette

Date

2013 Birthday

STORIES TO WARM A *Woman's* HEART

True Stories of Hope and Inspiration

EDITED BY JAMES STUART BELL

Guideposts

Stories to Warm a Woman's Heart

ISBN-10: 0-8249-4500-X
ISBN-13: 978-0-8249-4500-8

Published by Guideposts
16 East 34th Street
New York, New York 10016
Guideposts.org

Distributed by Ideals Publications, a Guideposts company
2630 Elm Hill Pike, Suite 100
Nashville, Tennessee 37214

Guideposts and *Ideals* are registered trademarks of Guideposts.

Cover and interior design by Thinkpen Design, Inc., www.thinkpendesign.com
Cover art/photo by Shutterstock
Typeset by Thinkpen Design, Inc.

Printed and bound in China
10 9 8 7 6 5 4 3 2 1

Contents

Introduction

We all have women that we admire—the ones who are gracious and loving, who light up a room with their presence and are always available when a friend calls. Women Proverbs 31 describes as being "joyful, faithful, wise."

This heartwarming collection is full of encouraging stories of women like that, striving to embody those same qualities—joy, faith, wisdom—and living life to the fullest.

They may be full-time mothers, have busy careers, volunteer at their church or in their communities. They may take care of their own parents while still trying to manage busy households, find time to connect with their husbands, and nurture their relationship with the Lord, not to mention find a few quiet moments to pursue their own interests.

They're an inspiration and a delight to be around. They know how to cherish the most important parts of their lives and to sacrifice their time and money. They grieve with their friends and don't shy away from the hardships in their lives. They celebrate the gifts they've been given and glory in the beauty of each day.

Whether you're an aunt, a girlfriend, a mother, daughter, wife, or friend, you'll find inspiration and comfort in these pages and cherish this warm celebration of women and what matters most to them.

Pink Is for Hope

BY DARLENE GARDNER

B ells chime softly as I open a door wreathed in pink roses. Pink letters spell out a welcome sign—LOVELY LADY. Soon I'll be greeted by some very special women. "My ladies," I call them. They mean the world to me. So does this shop. Yet if I had my druthers, I would close it down tomorrow, after over three decades. Let me explain.

Twenty-five years ago, I was a young nursing student in California, full of idealistic dreams. I didn't know where life would take me, but like many students, I felt a desire to make a difference. I volunteered to help with a breast cancer support group that met at the hospital. Week after week women of all ages opened their hearts. Some spoke of side effects from chemo; others discussed the challenges of juggling family responsibilities with treatments. But they had one thing in common—feeling like they lost their sense of normalcy when they lost their hair.

"It's like I have no privacy," one woman said. "One look at my head and everyone knows what's wrong."

"I can't even find a decent wig," said another. "Nothing looks like 'me.'"

Just a few weeks earlier, I'd accompanied my friend Carol on a trip to find a wig. Chemo had robbed her of her beautiful golden locks. We went all over town. Finally we ended up in a costume shop. Suffering from a serious disease, Carol was lumped in with people getting dressed up for Halloween! It broke my heart.

Now, listening to these women, I discovered many of them had had similar bad experiences looking for scarves, clothes, and even prosthetics. "I felt like a science experiment," said one.

Finally, one night driving home from the meeting, I turned to the Lord. *There must be some way to help these women. Show me how.*

My mom had taught me to sew, so at least I could make scarves. And when it came to fitting and styling wigs, I'd attended classes for wig cutting. What if I opened a shop for them? A place where women experiencing breast cancer could be given undivided attention and feel, at least for a time, normal. A haven of sorts where they could find prosthetics, jewelry, clothes, and wigs. (There would be nothing Halloweenish about it.) I found a cozy rental space and set up a shop called Bare Necessities. I took to my new mission—making every square inch welcoming. Wigs of every color and style were displayed on mannequins. Saucy hats and scarves in every shade lined ivory dressers. I hung verses on the walls. An open antique chest was home to inspirational books and pamphlets on breast cancer. I wanted women to feel as comfortable here as they did in a tearoom.

Word spread quickly. "Finally!" cried one of my first women. "A place where I can shop and sit and chat with other women facing cancer. God bless you!"

Another woman was shy at first. "I don't know if I have the strength to beat this," she admitted.

"Yes you do!" I said. "Just have faith." She left my shop with her head wrapped in a teal scarf and kept in touch with me throughout her treatment—today she's cancer-free! After a few months this little spot became a second home for women with cancer, a place where they could retreat from the burdens of illness. I'd found my life's work.

I spent over a decade in California, catering to my ladies. Then I headed east to North Carolina to care for my elderly parents. There I opened a new shop. I named it Lovely Lady, after my lovely mother who bestowed her skills on me. Today, I've added inspirational DVDs and CDs to the chest. Bouquets of fresh pink and crimson roses stand on every side table. Two rooms are beauty parlors with salon-style chairs and full-length mirrors. Everywhere there is pink. Pink, the color of triumph over breast cancer, the color of hope. The sitting room boasts two overstuffed couches where women can sit and chat. One day every month a cancer support group meets in the shop. I laugh and cry with my ladies, but most of all I listen. I draw inspiration from their struggles, strength from their stories.

Beverly, a spunky photographer, came to me when she first started losing her hair. "I'm looking for scarves," she said. "I don't think wigs are for me." Then she found the perfect wig to match the soft hairstyle she'd worn before her chemo treatments.

Other women are up for a change. One gal who'd just finished a treatment came into the shop feeling ill, but her sense of humor was intact. "Let's try something new today! I always wanted to be a blonde!"

At five o'clock the bells chime once more as I close the brass-trimmed door to the Lovely Lady. I softly say the same prayer every day: *Lord, please let there be a cure for breast cancer, so I can close my shop for good. But in the meantime help me make each woman feel like the lovely lady she is.*

A Lovely Life

The beauty of a woman
must be seen from in her eyes,
Because that is the doorway to her heart,
the place where love resides....
It is the caring that she lovingly gives,
the passion that she shows,
And the beauty of a woman
with passing years—only grows!

AUDREY HEPBURN

A Better Me!

BY TAMMIE TEMPLE

I waited that Saturday morning in April with butterflies in my stomach. My special guest were about to arrive. A month earlier I'd learned I'd won the New Year, New You contest. Though the people at Guideposts said I'd been chosen because I showed the most promise of all the entrants, I couldn't quite believe it. My self-esteem was at an all-time low, my weight was at an all-time high, and I certainly didn't feel like a winner.

Any minute the Guideposts Dream Team of lifestyle change coaches would be knocking at my door. I'd seen their photos in a previous *Guideposts* issue. I could picture the four of them charging into my house, ready for their mission, which was, as the contest announcement put it, "to develop a personalized healthy living plan" for me. Lord knows, I'd prayed for it and needed it!

It wasn't that I wasn't grateful for the many blessings in my life. I was married to my high school sweetheart, Greg, a marriage still going strong after twenty-five years. We had two wonderful sons, K.C. and Chris. We were building our dream house. I'd gotten a hard-earned college degree (I'd gone back to school at thirty-six and graduated at forty). I was a sixth-grade teacher. I had extended family, numerous friends, and a terrific church family.

But I had plenty of problems too. My weight had been an issue since childhood, and it was a major factor in my health problems—foot and back pain (exacerbated by being on my feet all day teaching), pre-hypertension, and pre-diabetes. I was only forty-two, much too young to be having so many physical issues. I knew I needed to get healthier, but where would I start? After all, I'd tried nearly every diet out there.

Physical fitness—or lack thereof—was another issue. Before the contest, I'd tried once again to get into shape by walking. I could barely walk a mile at first. I'd reared two athletic sons, soccer players who ran up and down the field; and I yearned to be able to run with them. After a long day at school and helping out with activities like the children's group at church, I was done. I had to decline when my coworker Dianne invited me to work out with her after school.

The problem I struggled with most was my negative thinking. It was at the root of all my other issues. Even with so many blessings in my life, I often felt like the world was crashing down on me. It was as if all the insults that had been leveled at me about my weight over the years had eaten away at my soul. I doubted my willpower, even doubted my faith was strong enough to make the changes in my life I knew I had to make.

At last a car pulled into the drive. I flung open the door. The Dream Team was here! There was a flurry of hugs and introductions. I recognized them all—Theresa Rowe, fitness expert; Kevin Carroll, motivational speaker; Rebecca Katz, chef and nutritionist; and Julie Hadden, my favorite contestant from *The Biggest Loser*. Someone said, "Tammie, are you ready to change your life?"

"I'm ready!" Time for the Dream Team to get to work.

Rebecca took on the huge challenge of teaching me how to buy and cook healthy food. She almost fainted when she looked in my pantry. I don't think she'd ever seen so many boxes of Hamburger Helper outside of a grocery store. She showed me how to read food labels, so I'd know the nutritional content and what to avoid, like high-fructose corn syrup and partially hydrogenated oils.

"Cut out processed and fried foods," she said, "and ramp up the fruits and vegetables."

But what would I feed Greg and the boys? They weren't big on vegetables. "I'm just trying to cook what they like," I explained. Rebecca wasn't buying it.

"If you want to change, you can't fall back on what you've always done. You need to make conscious choices," she said. "It won't kill your family to get off the fried stuff. Eating healthier will help all of you live longer. That's what you want for those you love, right?"

Of course! I just hadn't thought of it like that.

Kevin is known as Mr. Positivity, and I could see why. He exuded positive energy. "It's great that you want to make lifestyle changes. You've gotta aim high," Kevin said. "The way to reach a big goal is to set smaller goals leading up to it. Achieve one goal, then go for the next. When you reach a goal, reward yourself—but not with food."

Instead, he suggested going to a movie with Greg or taking a break from housework and spending some quiet time with God. What really got me was that Kevin said *when* I reached a goal. Not if, when.

I was intimidated by Theresa at first. She's in fantastic shape and serious about fitness. I thought she would be like those scary, in-your-face trainers I'd seen on TV; but she turned out to be deeply spiritual—a soul trainer. When I admitted I hated to exercise, Theresa wasn't fazed. "Don't think of it as a chore. Think of it as a time to be with the Lord and to praise Him," she said. "Say you're power walking. Look around at all the Lord has created and give thanks." Exercise as a form of prayer? Now that I could relate to!

I felt like I knew Julie already from watching *The Biggest Loser* and reading her cover story in *Guideposts*. In person, she was even more inspiring. She gave me lots of tips, like keeping a journal to record every calorie I put in my mouth as well as calories I burned. She challenged me to ask myself why I was reaching for food: *Am I really hungry? Or am I bored? upset? stressed?*

The most important lesson Julie taught me had nothing to do with eating or exercise and everything to do with my emotional and spiritual well-being. That afternoon a photographer came to take pictures of me in front of our azaleas. "I hope you have your wide-angle lens," I joked.

Julie pounced on me like a dog on a June bug. "Do you realize what you do to your mind-set when you say things like that, Tammie? You've got to cut that out. Now I want you to say, 'I am worthy of this opportunity.'"

I opened my mouth, but I couldn't get the words out. Tears sprang to my eyes. I hadn't felt worthy of anything for so long. In fact, I'd lived my life feeling just the opposite. "Say it, Tammie."

It took me a few tries but I finally got it out: "I am worthy." Whoa. I could feel myself standing taller, facing the world with more confidence. Who knew three simple words could be so powerful?

It was an intense weekend. Sunday evening my Dream Team coaches went home. They'd be in touch regularly, but now it was up to me to put all the good information they'd given me into practice.

First, I found a workout partner. Like Theresa advised, I chose someone who liked to exercise every day, so her commitment would strengthen mine. I joined the gym and met Dianne there every day after school. I set my first small goal: running a mile. Dianne cheered me on from the next treadmill, "Just one more minute, Tammie. You can do anything for a minute!" The day I ran my first mile, I don't know who cried harder, Dianne or I.

My next challenge was eating healthy. It certainly took a lot longer to shop when I read the labels. But choosing fruits, vegetables, and lean protein was worth it. *I'm worth it*, I reminded myself. My men were taken aback when I declared our kitchen a no-fry zone, but they got into it once they realized food that's good for them could still taste good.

Regular exercise worked wonders. I had the energy to keep up with the kids at church even after a long day at school. I increased the distance I ran to three miles. Then I set another goal: running a 5K. Chris decided he'd do the race with me, so we trained together over the summer. He ran figure eights around me, that smart aleck, but what a joy it was to be working out with my son!

Of course, obstacles cropped up—the pizza party for my mom's birthday, trips out of town, those five weeks when I hit a plateau and didn't lose an ounce. But I drew on the support of the Dream Team, my family, and friends and powered through. Most of all, I drew on my faith. It struck me that all those excuses I used to make—*I'm just meant to be big, I'm too tired to exercise, my guys won't go for vegetables*—were forms of negative thinking. I was telling myself "I can't" when God was trying to show me I could. As Dianne pointed out when I got down on myself, "You graduated college with a 4.0 GPA while working full time. You accomplished that; you can accomplish anything you set your mind to." Like that 5K. I ran all the way to the finish line. When I told my class, one of the kids, bless his heart, said, "Awesome! Mrs. Temple, you should try out to be a Dallas Cowboy cheerleader!" That's not my next goal, but I sure like that line of thinking.

I'm reminded of one of my favorite Scriptures, from Hebrews: "Let us lay aside every weight...and let us run with patience the race that is set before us, looking unto Jesus the author and finisher of our faith." (Hebrews 12:1-2 KJV) I never would've dreamed I'd be able to get healthy, lose more than sixty pounds or run five miles (that's what I'm up to now). Just goes to show what's possible when you set aside the weight of your negative thinking and see the potential God sees in you!

Reach Your Potential

God created us with an overwhelming desire to soar. Our desire to develop and use every ounce of potential He's placed in us is not egotistical. He designed us to be tremendously productive and "to mount up with wings like eagles," realistically dreaming of what He can do with our potential.

CAROL KENT

A Gift of New Life

BY KARIN SCREWS

Perhaps it wasn't love at first sight, but it came mighty close. Keith and I were freshmen at the University of Georgia when we met. I was majoring in child development, planning to become a teacher. Keith's major was animal science; he hoped to raise cattle someday. The future seemed to hold nothing but promise.

I was attracted by Keith's good looks, gentleness, and perfect manners. But the most appealing thing about Keith was a love of life that seemed to shine through everything he did. He loved sports; he had been a star athlete in high school. He loved keeping fit. He loved the red earth and tranquil ponds and pine woods of rural Georgia. He loved people, and people were drawn to him too. When we were married the year after we finished college, we felt sure we would live happily ever after.

Both of us wanted to stay in southern Georgia. I got a job teaching behavior-disordered children in the small town of Baxley. Keith was selling farm supplies and looking forward to raising his own cattle. We lived modestly, but material things were not important to us. We wanted to start a family but were in no hurry.

Three years went by. Then abdominal pains led Keith to consult a doctor. We were told he had cancer.

It was a tremendous shock. How could someone who seemed so healthy be facing such a deadly enemy? The doctors tried to sound optimistic. It was a slow-growing type of non-Hodgkin's lymphoma, they said, usually associated with much older people.

After the diagnosis, Keith wanted to be closer to his family in Swainsboro, so we bought a few acres of pastureland nearby with a tiny farmhouse, weather-beaten and run-down, but big enough for two. We got a few handsome red-and-white Simmental cattle and set about raising a small herd.

Then Keith began chemotherapy. We hoped and prayed. We knew many other people were praying too.

It was hard not to ask why this was happening to us. Gradually we learned that God's answer to such a question is not an explanation. His answer lies in just two words: "Trust Me."

One of our doctors suggested what I now think was part of God's plan for us. Since the chemotherapy could render Keith sterile, the doctor said we might consider storing some of Keith's semen in a sperm bank. We decided to do this.

As the months went by, we faced our situation as best we could. We had heard of cases where serious illness drove couples apart, but our problem brought us closer together. Keith did not flinch at the thought of dying. His faith was his salvation; he was sure of going to heaven. But he hated the possibility of leaving me, and I dreaded it too.

Both of us wanted the experience of parenthood very much. So when Keith was feeling better, we decided that despite the cancer and our uncertain future we would try to bring new life into the world.

My doctor said that perhaps our best chance would be with in vitro fertilization. In this procedure the woman's egg is fertilized by the man's sperm outside the body and then implanted in the uterus. There is only a 20 percent chance of pregnancy. To improve those odds, the reproductive endocrinologist, Dr. Edouard Servy, decided to implant five fertilized eggs. No one expected more than one or possibly two to survive. Four did! Dr. Cecil Sharp, the neonatologist who cared for them, later had an explanation: "I think those babies received a special blessing from God." I think so too.

It was a difficult pregnancy though; I had a tendency to go into labor much too soon. At twenty-six weeks I was admitted into University Hospital in Augusta and kept on bed rest for more than two months. Even with labor-suppressant drugs, contractions started four times. Each time, they were headed off by a devoted team of ten specialists—they called themselves the quad squad—whose kindness and cheerfulness supported me during those nerve-racking weeks.

Meanwhile, Keith's condition suddenly deteriorated. He entered Emory University Hospital in Atlanta, about 150 miles from Augusta. This was hard for both of us. In all our married life we had never been separated for any length of time. Dan Johnson, a professional photographer who had been Keith's college roommate, made a videotape of me for Keith to reassure him that I was okay and to try to help him stay positive.

In November the cancer reached Keith's liver. His one desire now was that he would live to see his babies born. His doctors tried valiantly to build up his strength to make this possible, and they succeeded. On December 17, our babies were delivered by cesarean section while Keith sat beside me in the operating room.

First came a boy weighing 3 pounds 14 ounces: Robert Jared Screws. After Robert Jared came his three sisters: Brianna Rae, 3 pounds 1 ounce; Brinsley Faye, 3 pounds 13 ounces; and Buckley Lenay, 4 pounds 2 ounces. All were tiny, but they were strong, healthy babies. In the hallway outside the operating room, friends and relatives wept and cheered as the quad squad wheeled them by, one by one, in their incubators.

The babies stayed in the hospital about a month. Keith went there too, for more chemotherapy, and the nurses took one or two babies at a time to his room for a visit. That seemed to help him more than the medication.

Then came a wonderful surprise. When we were ready to go home, we learned that a physicians' fund had provided a brand-new van for us, complete with four infant car seats.

Keith was waiting for us at home, frail now and in constant pain, but also very happy. That first night, wanting to be alone with each other and the babies, we shooed all our eager helpers away. But by the next morning we were clamoring for them to come back!

The whole community of Swainsboro and surrounding towns united in trying to help us. Countless women offered to baby-sit. Members of Keith's high school class prepared dinners for us twice a week. All sorts of fund-raising events were organized. A Kroger store on Wilmington Island near Savannah donated a year's supply of diapers and other baby needs. That helped, because the quads required forty to fifty diapers a day!

A man named Ricky Stevens came to measure our farmhouse for central air conditioning but went away concerned that the house was too small for six people. That night he could not sleep; he felt that God was telling him to do something about our situation. He consulted Ken Warnock, a friend in real estate, and the two of them invited a group of Swainsboro businessmen to lunch. By the time lunch was over, they had enough pledges to begin building a new house.

There was a site on our land with a view of the pasture and grazing cattle. Our new house would be built there, a spacious home with five bedrooms—a master bedroom and one for each of the quads. Ricky called the project "Four a Brighter Day."

As spring came to Georgia, Keith's health continued to decline. Still, he took great delight in his four babies. In the mornings he would hold them and play with them and help feed them. He got to be good at handling two bottles at a time. Before we left home for a chemo treatment or doctor's appointment, Keith would spend time alone with each baby.

Later in the spring another operation was necessary, and complications followed. It became difficult for Keith to talk or breathe, and at last he lost consciousness. His final words to me were, "I love you."

The doctors put him on a respirator, but they said it was only a matter of hours. I sat beside him holding his hand and whispering, "Be at peace. Be at peace." And finally, on June 11, peace did come. He was thirty-two years old.

Life went on. Ground was broken for the new house on a blue-and-gold day in December. The quads were old enough to stand, and each was given a little gilded shovel to mark the occasion. Many friends and neighbors were there, and the mayor of Swainsboro put our feelings into words: "We hope that when these babies are grown, they will look at this house and understand how much their father was respected and admired by everyone who knew him."

I have gone back to teaching. Devoted friends and relatives and fully qualified helpers take good care of the quads while I am away.

People ask me sometimes if these experiences have left me embittered. One thing I try to remember is the apostle Paul's tremendous assurance that "all things work together for good to them that love God" (Romans 8:28 KJV). I truly believe that. Without Keith's illness we never would have recognized the amazing goodness that lies in people. The outpouring of love and compassion and caring that surrounded us was almost beyond belief.

Far from being weakened, my faith has been strengthened in the goodness and wisdom of God. One life was taken away from me, but four other lives were given to me to sustain and to comfort me. Facing death with Keith made me realize how precious life is. I cherish it and am grateful for it every single day.

Amazing Goodness

*God's good from life's bad is one of the most
liberating concepts in the entire Word of God.
We'll never be free until we truly believe that
God can do something with anything.
God has promised to bring good out of anything
we encounter as long as we love Him and if
we allow Him to use it for His purpose.*

BETH MOORE

Extreme Makeover
(Attitude Edition)

BY KAREN BARBER

Gordon worked his crowbar between the base molding and the wall in the upstairs bedroom of our beach house. He gave it a jerk and the baseboard popped loose. He moved on to the next piece of molding. He was like a machine. It wasn't yet 8:00 a.m.—the first morning of a four-day job installing oak laminate floor in two bedrooms and a hallway—and already my husband was sweating. Yet he seemed to be enjoying it.

I'd just made my way upstairs after downing my second cup of tea. Actually I'd been jarred from my reverie by Gordon hollering for me to bring him the vacuum. Now I was sitting on the floor, adjusting my knee pads, and watching baseboards pile up around the room. Gordon scowled at me. *What was that about?* He didn't even need the vacuum yet. And there wasn't anything for me to do....

"Take these down to the van, so we can haul them to the dump," he said, thrusting an armload of baseboards at me. *Now he's telling me what to do?* Last year Gordon and a buddy had laid a laminate floor downstairs. But the buddy wasn't available for this job, so I'd been dumb enough to volunteer. I gathered up the remaining pieces of wood and headed downstairs. If his buddy were here, Gordon wouldn't be ordering him around. Had we really been married for thirty-five years?

We were so different! Gordon is a model of efficiency. He even walks quickly, making me tell him to slow down when I can't keep up. He leaves before 6:00 a.m. to get to work as an operations manager with the phone company. Even there he gets paid to keep things running. Sometimes when I look into his eyes, I see fingers snapping. *C'mon, let's keep it moving.*

Me? I'm a writer. I work from home on my own schedule. Sometimes I sit at my desk with my eyes closed and let time drift by, thinking, contemplating, and imagining. Occasionally—like when we were raising our three sons—our differences complemented each other. He'd play with the boys till he tired them out, and then I'd read to them. At other times, like on this remodeling project, Gordon could seem overbearing. Why did he have to be in such a hurry? And so...industrious?

A few years ago I'd begun praying daily, hoping God might show me a way to bridge our differences. *Help me to love, honor, and respect Gordon; and help us to understand each other.* I had the love, honor, and respect part down pretty well. Now if we could only figure out the understanding thing.

I went back upstairs, forcing myself to jog the last few steps. Gordon had another job waiting. "Help me roll up the carpet," he said.

I tried. The carpet wouldn't budge. He pulled a blade from his tool belt and slashed the carpet into two sections, one smaller than the other. I still couldn't lift it. Gordon didn't speak. He picked up the rolls of carpet, one under each arm, and marched downstairs with them, almost triumphantly. I sat on the floor, my back against the wall and my legs stretched out in front of me, giving my knees a rest. I might have let my eyes close for a second because next thing I knew Gordon was standing in the doorway staring at me.

"What?" I said defensively.

"Honey, I know there are things you can't do," he said. "But while I'm doing those things, maybe you could look around and find something else to do."

"I'm doing the best I can," I snapped. "I'm just not as strong as you." I was about to let him have it when I noticed his matted hair and his shirt, damp with sweat. I could hear him catching his breath. He was really working hard. I buttoned my mouth into a frown and swallowed the rest of what I had to say.

Gordon began attacking the carpet tack strips with the crowbar. I got up, pressing the palm of my hand against the subflooring. My hand ground into a thick layer of...sand! It had sifted down through the carpet over the years. That's why Gordon had wanted the vacuum. I preferred a broom and dustpan and went to the kitchen to get my tools. Soon I was busy sweeping half a beach into a pile. It was quiet, satisfying work, almost contemplative compared to what Gordon was doing. Maybe there was something I could do on my own and even do in my own way. Maybe even enjoy it.

At exactly 11:30 a.m. Gordon said, "Time for lunch." We made sandwiches and ate them on the deck, the silence broken only by the occasional "Pass the chips." Gordon seemed lost in thought, like he was calculating something.

I was leisurely crunching on a chip when Gordon said, "Time to start laying the floor." He picked up two boxes of flooring and started up the stairs. I tried to pick up a box. No way. I followed empty-handed. Gordon put the boxes on the far end of the room then went down for more. I opened the boxes and tore off the plastic, then sat down and read the directions. Gordon doesn't always take the time to read directions, or need them. But I'll read just about anything.

The instructions said to mix boards from several boxes in case there were color differences. That made sense. I started piling planks from alternating boxes on the floor so they'd be within easy reach. Gordon came up with the other boxes, looked at my work, and nodded approvingly. I couldn't help but smile back.

Gordon showed me how the planks had a tongue on one side and groove on the other, how you bent the plank back and clicked it into the channel then pushed it down so it locked in place. We worked together, me holding one end steady and Gordon jiggling the other. I saw how the planks started out with a big crack separating them, but with some work they were smooth and tight—like they were one. I looked at my husband and suddenly I wanted to kiss his brow.

We fell into a good rhythm and the afternoon sped along. By 7:00 p.m. the front bedroom was about three-fourths done. It looked great. I felt a swell of pride. Gordon fished a limp piece of paper out of his pocket, unfolded it, and announced, "I think we can quit for the night. This will put us right on schedule."

"Schedule?" I said.

Gordon nodded. "I was worried because I'm not as good at this as my buddy. I wasn't sure I could do it in four days without him. So I made this timetable."

"Oh," I said meekly. It never dawned on me he might be working from a plan. I thought it was his mania for efficiency. Gordon raised his arm and wiped sweat from his face, his biceps glistening. He looked good, strong, and handsome with his tool belt hung across his hips, like a tall, lean gunslinger.

There was something else I admired. I recalled how he'd known what to do each step of the way and how much I'd learned from him. I thought about that prayer I said for our marriage. I'd asked to understand my husband. My prayer had been answered in an unexpected way—a home-improvement project turned into a self-improvement one. I gave Gordon a hug.

"Hey, handsome. You're one strong dude. Where'd you learn to lay flooring like that? I'm impressed."

Gordon draped his arm around my shoulders and said, "Thanks. I couldn't have done it without my partner."

Home Improvement

Having someone who understands you is home.
Having someone who loves you is belonging.
Having both is a blessing.

UNKNOWN

The Priority Principle

BY JANE KISE

Friday afternoon a stack of paper six inches thick sat on my desk. I laid a ruler on the top sheet, using it to keep my place while I checked the numbers. I was a senior financial analyst at the biggest bank in Minneapolis, and my division was responsible for a billion dollars. Every number had to add up. But that's not what worried me. My mind kept wandering to a bigger problem—what my manager would say when I told him I was expecting my first child.

My due date meant I'd miss next year's entire budget season. Dan, my hard-driving boss, would never understand. He was so work-obsessed he practically ate three meals a day at his desk. His hair was prematurely gray. You could almost measure how close we were to budget deadlines by how deep he frowned. Today he looked utterly exhausted, rushing to pack his briefcase full of work to take home. *Does he have any time for his family?* I wondered. *Will I?*

I thought of talking to Mike, my team leader. Mike went home at five o'clock almost every night. He had two boys and a wife who went to school in the evenings. "I've got to be on time for the second shift at home," he joked. His cubicle was plastered with pictures of his children on the jungle gym he had built for them and the T-ball team he coached and the family dressed up for church on Easter.

Even before I knew I was pregnant, Mike had said to me, "You can get your work done and leave on time. Just figure out what's important to you. Everything else follows from there." But Dan was my real boss. You kept his hours.

I couldn't postpone our talk much longer; I had to start wearing maternity dresses. I'd been pinning my skirts where the buttons wouldn't reach.

Pushing aside the stack of paper, I got up. Just then Dan's assistant dropped a memo off at my desk. We were supposed to run a new set of numbers on our report. "Have them to me by Monday," Dan had written.

I glanced at the clock. The mainframe computer was already shut down for the weekend. Making the changes by Monday meant doing them by hand on Saturday. I heard the angry voices of my teammates in Mike's office, so I headed over.

"Where's Dan now?" someone asked.

"He had to leave for an emergency dentist appointment. We're supposed to send the numbers to his house."

"It'll take us at least eight hours to plug in those numbers, and the figures might not even be right," I said.

Another analyst said, "Dan did this just to make us work a Saturday—"

"We don't need to," Mike said, smiling as he leaned back in his chair. "I'll run a program first thing Monday when the computer comes back up. And I'll explain things to Dan on Tuesday. The extra day means there won't be any mistakes."

I had a terrible weekend. Mike probably played ball with his boys, but I barely slept. After this, how would Dan view my maternity leave? *Dear God,* I prayed, *can I have a career and still be the kind of mother I want to be?*

On Monday, Mike finished running the program before I came in. I checked the information for my division, skipping lunch to go over it all. I kept envisioning Dan exploding in anger the next morning.

Tuesday I arrived before the rest of the team. I poured a cup of coffee and sat in my cubicle, hiding behind computer printouts. Dan stalked in. "Get in my office," he said without looking at me. "Now!"

I sat down across from him, sitting on my shaking hands. His eyes narrowed. "I wanted those reports yesterday so I could get my notes ready. If that means working on a Saturday, that's normal at your level of responsibility. Instead, you deliberately disobeyed me."

I struggled to hold back my tears. That was when Mike breezed in with the new report. "Here you go, Dan," he said, plopping it on his desk. "Guaranteed accurate, down to the decimal. To me that was worth taking an extra day."

Dan flipped through the pages. "Why didn't you work on Saturday to finish this?"

"It seemed like a huge waste when we could just use the computer and get it right," Mike said, "so we waited till Monday. I had to follow my own judgment."

Dan stared at the top page for a long while, then nodded. At that moment the tension went out of the room like air going out of a balloon. We spent the rest of the morning helping Dan prepare for the meeting. He even cracked a smile!

That afternoon, he called us into his office and said, "The executive committee felt our presentation was the most thorough." We all congratulated each other as if there'd never been a problem.

Later, finally on my way to talk to Dan about my pregnancy, I stopped by Mike's cubicle. There he was, working as hard as ever, surrounded by the photos of his boys, his T-ball team, and his family on Easter Sunday. They weren't a distraction; they were his inspiration. That's why he didn't make time-wasting decisions or worry about his status and office politics. He had his priorities right: God, family, then work. And because of that he was good at all three.

"Thanks, Mike, for everything you did."

"It was just a report," he said.

"No. It was more than that," I said. I'd gotten my priorities straight. Now I was ready to tell my boss the good news.

My Prayer

*Heavenly Father, please give me the ability
to see things as You see them. Help me to
understand the importance of eternal things,
and remind me not to focus so much energy
on temporal things. May I be diligent in my home,
yet more faithful to nurture the most important
part of my home...my family. Amen.*

KIM BOYCE

Spread the Joy

BY KATHIE LEE GIFFORD

When Cassidy was little, our neighbors in Connecticut must have thouhgt we were a bunch of nuts. In the morning when two-year-old Cassidy came up to me saying, "Hosanna, Mommy, hosanna," I'd say, "Okay." And out we'd traipse onto our deck where we'd march around singing, "This is the day the Lord has made. Let us rejoice and be glad in it! Hosanna! Hosanna!" I'm sure people all the way in New Jersey heard us.

But I didn't care what they thought. I believe worship should be fun and exciting, so children can embrace it. After all, David leaped and danced before the Lord with all his might, and he sang out with joy.

We Christians don't do that enough. Often we're all so terrified of what somebody's going to say. But if you love the Lord, you should show it.

"The joy of the Lord is your strength." That's Nehemiah 8:10, a verse that has always been important to me. People ask me where I get my energy. But what most people perceive as energy is really strength of spirit. It comes from the joy of knowing God, loving Him, and being loved by Him. It's so simple we sometimes stumble past it.

I first began my walk with Jesus at age twelve when I came home and found my mom and my little sister, Michie, crying together in the living room. Immediately I sensed these weren't tears of sadness, but of some more momentous emotion.

Mom had been flipping between TV channels when she came across a Billy Graham crusade. She had always scoffed at this sort of event before. But that night as she watched, she had spontaneously fallen to her knees and asked God to come into her life. My sister joined her. Then I arrived and was deeply affected as well.

Not long after, I saw a Christian film called *The Restless Ones*. At its conclusion the pastor asked us to come forward and receive Christ. It was an electrifying and life-changing experience.

In the teenage years that followed, my commitment only deepened. God seemed to be saying to me, "Kathie, everyone has to make choices. Choose My way, and I will help you make something beautiful of your life." By then my dad was a Christian too, and over and over I got the message: Shine in the light of God's love; be a blessing, not a burden; and love others. I was taught to bloom where I was planted, to find joy in whoever I was or whatever I became, and to spread that joy generously and enthusiastically.

My husband, Frank, says I get too enthusiastic sometimes. "I can just see your motor overheating," he says, laughing. But I think if you love the Lord and love others as yourself, the Holy Spirit gives you a natural exuberance in which you say the right thing at the right time. Scripture tells us that perfect love casts out all fear. If I believe God loves me perfectly, then I won't be afraid of life. I won't be afraid to try new things, to look foolish, or to fail. And if I do sometimes fall on my face, so what? Even though we make mistakes daily, the Bible says that God's mercy is fresh for us every morning.

When I first started working with Regis Philbin, who was hosting WABC-TV's *The Morning Show,* I knew he had a reputation of teasing his cohosts. But I repeated to myself, "The joy of the Lord is my strength," and it kept me from feeling intimidated. I was able to relax and throw wisecracks right back at Regis. The show came to be called *Live with Regis and Kathie Lee* and it became unscripted, spontaneous, and outrageous. Regis and I became great friends. Knowing we did some good was so rewarding to us. We didn't cure cancer or AIDS, but a lot of healing comes through laughter. If we could be a part of such a process, we're grateful.

My life hasn't been all fun. Michie, my sister, almost died at the age of twenty-three from acute ulcerative colitis. She had an ileostomy and lay in a coma. As I sat at her bedside, I silently cursed God for the unfairness of it all. Why should my sister have to go through such agony? At that moment Michie opened her eyes, looked right at me, and said, "Kathie, don't curse God; thank Him. This bag means I get to live!" It was one of the most humbling—and elating—moments of my life.

Some time ago I learned a disturbed man had threatened to harm me. Even in jail and serving two life terms for another crime, he continued to write me letters. From the start I decided I was not going to worry and let this spoil my life. I have had to hand certain things over to God. It's the living out of my faith that makes me a believer. God doesn't just get rid of hardship or suffering; He heals in the midst of it.

My reading of the Scripture has taught me that people who love the Lord don't automatically rise to the top in business or beat cancer overnight. At times, faith means enduring surgery or chemotherapy or any number of other difficult experiences. It means tapping into a deeper dimension when loved ones suffer terrible illness or misfortune.

One of the lowest points of my life was when I went to Hollywood in the 1970s, trying to carve out a career for myself. One gloomy afternoon, sitting in my apartment after many rejections, I realized I was down to my last few dollars. "Lord," I prayed, "if I don't get a job by this time next week, I'll go home to Maryland and be a florist or an interior designer."

That week I was offered parts in five commercials. I took that flurry of activity as my answer. Later some people said, "What's a nice Christian girl like you doing in show business?" My reply was "Aren't nice Christian men in the plumbing business?" We can't all be ministers or priests or rabbis. But we are supposed to be the sweet fragrance of Jesus wherever we are, whatever our occupation.

I've never felt apologetic about my faith or my career; it's the Lord I want to please, not critics or "religious" people. When asked, "Don't you find it hard to be a Christian in the entertainment business?" I answer, "No, I would find it impossible not to be one. How does anyone get through the day without the Lord?"

That's why I jumped in wholeheartedly to join Cassidy and her five-year-old brother, Cody, when we marched around the deck doing our hosannas. They were learning from their earliest days that God loves them and has a plan for their lives. The joy of the Lord is their strength too.

Radiant Joy

God made you in His image, to bear His likeness,
His imprint. When Christ dwells in your heart,
radiating the pure light of His love through
your humanity, you'll discover who you are
and what you were intended to be.
There is no other joy that is more complete.

WENDY MOORE

Long Road to Calnali

BY JUANA ORELLAN WATSON

My father had brought the crumpled papers home. They had been packed around pots that were sold in the market, and scraps of this sort served as our family's rags and toilet paper. One of the fragments caught my eye, and I smoothed out a page that must have been torn from a magazine. It showed a beautiful tree, laden with shiny ornaments and surrounded by colorfully wrapped boxes. In the background was a fat man with a white beard, wearing a red outfit.

As an eight-year-old girl living in Calnali, a remote village in the Sierra Madre Mountains of Mexico, I could make no sense of the picture. What were those packages? Who was that person with a beard?

I asked my mother, but she didn't know. I took the picture to my teacher, who answered, "His name is Santa Claus. He brings presents to children at Christmas."

I was excited. "Will he bring gifts to children in Calnali? To me and my friends?"

My teacher sighed. "Santa comes to children in rich families. He never comes to such a poor village."

I still remember how stung I was by the unfairness of this revelation. I determined that someday I would get Santa Claus to come to Calnali.

My schooling in Calnali finished when I was ten. But I was bright and curious and wanted more. My grandfather, a great influence in my life, convinced my parents to send me away to school. We learned of a boarding school in Tlaxcala that was free to certain needy rural children. My father earned an extra five dollars by cutting and selling coffee beans so we would have money for the trip.

My father and I made the grueling two-day trip on horseback and by bus. When we arrived at the school, I had to take an entrance exam. My father did not understand that passing this exam was a prerequisite to enrollment. He was already on his way home when the school informed me that out of a thousand children who took the exam, only fifty could be admitted. I was not among the fifty. I would have to leave.

It was an awful predicament. Contacting my parents was impossible; there were no phones in Calnali and a letter could take months. Besides, I knew I might never get a chance to leave Calnali again. So I began to fend for myself.

Though the school would not accept responsibility for me, a few teachers and students took pity. I slept on the floor; I ate leftover food in exchange for dishwashing. Although not allowed in the classroom, I stood listening outside the doors. I was frightened and often lonely, but determined. A year later,

I was accepted as a student in the seventh grade, and I learned and thrived.

After high school, I obtained a position as a police dispatcher in Mexico City. I saved enough money to travel to Europe and studied for two months at the Sorbonne. For a girl from a poor Mexican family, these were amazing experiences. I thanked God for my good fortune.

While working as a translator in the Mexico City airport, I met an American businessman who brought me to live in Columbus, Indiana. We married, but sadly the marriage ended in divorce. I then met and married Grant Watson. I had a lovely two-story home in a pleasant subdivision, a successful catering business, and a devoted husband and three healthy, happy children. I had escaped from the poverty of my origins. But the eight-year-old girl who cried because Santa would not come to a poor village still haunted me.

Each year I visited my parents, who, despite my pleas, would not leave their town. I felt troubled and frustrated. The village hadn't changed much since I had left. People continued to labor long and hard in the sugarcane or coffee fields and to bathe and wash clothes in the same river from which they got their drinking water. There was still no doctor. Women died in childbirth, and children died in infancy. People suffered from diseases that would have been easily treatable with rudimentary medical help.

I was particularly affected when I saw women my own age with whom I used to play as a child. Their hard lives, poor nutrition, and years of exhausting childbearing had made these women old before their time. If I had not left, I would have become one of them.

My beloved grandfather was dead, but I began to think about the philosophy he had taught me. "The life you live is not your own," he told me. "It belongs to God. And one day God will want it back. It won't be enough to say, 'Sorry, God, I didn't do much—my life didn't make a difference.'"

All my accomplishments seemed hollow. I wanted to make a difference. I just didn't know how.

Then a member of my church in Columbus, a surgeon, mentioned he was serving on a medical mission trip to Mexico. I went along as a translator. There, in a village much like Calnali, I saw how a medical team brought hope. Mothers wept with joy as children were healed; old people smiled as their pain was relieved.

This was the direction I had been seeking. This same mission group must go to Calnali! When I approached the directors with the idea, they told me it was beyond their resources—Calnali was too remote, too primitive. "But," they said, "there is another organization that might consider it." And that's how I found T.I.M.E. for Christ, Inc., a nondenominational medical mission group based in San Antonio, Texas.

Indeed, T.I.M.E. for Christ (Teaching, Intercession, Ministering, Evangelism) was willing to travel to more remote areas. But after checking maps and gathering information, even this intrepid group was daunted. Calnali was off the beaten track. Everything needed for the project would have to be brought in by truck. The only road leading there was difficult and dangerous, with muddy ruts and steep drop-offs.

Convincing T.I.M.E. that a visit to Calnali should be a priority became my obsession. I consulted the mayor of Calnali and the local priest to figure out the logistics. I brought back photographs of the town as well as statistics on how urgently help was needed. It took about two years, but I finally convinced T.I.M.E.'s directors it could be done.

Finally one December, my husband and I joined more than one hundred volunteer doctors, nurses, and medical technicians as trucks filled with supplies and equipment rumbled out of San Antonio at dawn. We drove for more than twenty hours. As we bounced over ruts and inched our way around treacherous mountain turns, I knew I wasn't the only one praying.

On the day after Christmas our caravan rolled into Calnali. The villagers lined the road, staring in amazement. My father was waiting to meet us, along with many others. I'll never forget the looks in the children's wide eyes. No, we hadn't brought Santa Claus, but we were bringing something better—friends.

We quickly set up for our week-long stay. The schoolhouse and its grounds were transformed into a medical clinic that included a pharmacy, a lab, and a surgery center.

Most Calnali residents had never seen a doctor in their lives. Many were frightened by the array of doctors and equipment, but those of us who spoke Spanish soothed their fears; and we distributed Bibles and balloons to the children. Long lines snaked around the school yard as people waited their turn.

Working from morning till nightfall, the team administered X-rays and performed lab tests and operations. A six-year-old girl's cleft palate was corrected; a man who had broken his foot six months earlier had the bones set; a ninety-two-year-old woman found relief from the hernia she had suffered for years. Dentists extracted decayed teeth, and about six thousand prescriptions were filled.

Grant was as moved as I was by the spontaneous expressions of gratitude from the villagers, bearing bananas and peppers as gifts, who came to my parents' house to thank us. Seeing the joy on their faces was worth all the exhausting work.

One day, while walking among the crowd waiting to see the doctors, I noticed a familiar face. My old schoolteacher! I cried as I put my arms around the frail, elderly man. Suffering from a respiratory infection, he was given antibiotics. Within days, his condition improved.

Later that week my old teacher and I laughed, remembering my childhood chagrin about Santa. "You kept following me around asking, 'But why won't Santa come here?'" he recalled. "And now you have brought a far better gift to us than Santa ever could have."

Yes, it was a gift, but not only to the people of Calnali. It was also a gift to God.

My Gift to God

If I can do some good today,
If I can serve along life's way,
If I can something helpful say,
Lord, show me how.

GRENVILLE KLEISER

Our Sunday Visitor

BY SHIRLEY McCLINTOCK

Boing...boing...boing... The kitchen clock was chiming seven when I finally heard Ken come through the front door, and I could have boinged him. Late for supper again. I shoved a casserole in the oven and fumed while Ken hung up his coat and visited with our sons, Steven and Tim.

I realized that my husband, an attorney with a busy general practice, couldn't usher every client out of his office at precisely five. But he didn't even try! If someone had a problem, he'd let him talk and talk and talk. Sometimes Ken didn't even charge the person, despite the fact that we needed the money.

When Ken strolled into the kitchen a few minutes later and asked, "Is dinner ready?" I exploded.

"No it isn't! Why should it be? I never have any idea when you're coming home!"

"Sorry," he apologized. "I had a late client." He looked around the kitchen, noting the exact stage of meal preparation with legal precision. "Can I help? Set the table or make a salad?"

"Just get out of here and leave me alone!" I ordered.

Bewildered, Ken retreated.

Three minutes later I changed my mind. "Come visit with me!" I demanded. But Ken was reading the newspaper and didn't hear.

Dinner, when we finally ate, was a silent affair. Lately, our marriage resembled an armed truce. The more I pleaded for openness and communication, the more silent and withdrawn Ken became. The more he withdrew, the angrier I got.

"Talk to me!" I'd plead with him. "I want to know what you think, what you feel!" I left my real plea unspoken: "Love me...let me know you truly love me."

All my life I'd longed for the kind of love that would wrap around me and keep me warm. My parents loved me and I'd experienced several revelations of God's love. But I wanted something more—something no one, not even my husband, seemed able to give. Was there some deep, dark secret to being loved? Did only a few chosen people experience it?

Our marriage was at the breaking point, but no one knew it—not our relatives, not our friends, not even our fellow church members. Outwardly we were a good Christian family. We attended church each week. Ken narrated the Easter cantata, and I occasionally sang solos. We practiced biblical hospitality— "Cheerfully share your home with those who need a meal" (1 Peter 4:9 TLB).

In fact, that's how Hall Moxley came into our lives. I felt so sorry for the poor man that I invited him home for Sunday dinner.

Ken and I had known Hall casually for years. Once he'd been a prominent cattleman and successful farmer, but his erratic, unpredictable behavior and poor business decisions had cost him everything. Bit by bit, he'd lost his cattle, his land, and even his family.

Eventually doctors discovered his problem—a massive brain tumor with roots reaching deep inside the brain. They'd been able to remove only part of it. Cobalt treatments helped but could only slow the tumor's growth temporarily.

A home-cooked meal wasn't much, but it was all I had to offer. Besides, it meant someone to talk to. Ken didn't talk to me anymore. Hall was considered a bit strange by some people, but so what? We could manage for one meal.

To our surprise, having him was fun! His compliments on the roast beef and angel food cake delighted me. "Mm! This food is so-o-o-o good!" he said over and over. With his elbow he poked Tim, who was gulping his dinner. "Slow down, boy! Take your time and enjoy this delicious meal."

Later Hall told us how God's love had sustained him through every crisis. Not even the doctors' ominous you-might-have-only-six-months-to-live shook his abiding faith or his desire to spread God's love to others. Hall's special concern was for the sick. He visited the hospital and nursing home every week.

"Only two things really hurt," he confided. "Losing my family and not being able to read the Bible like I used to. Sometimes it takes me an hour to work through ten verses of Scripture!"

Then he brightened. "But I can still love! And that's the most important thing there is."

Hall—always wearing the same brown cowboy-cut suit—became a regular Sunday guest. The boys considered him a best friend; he romped and played right along with them. He provided out-of-the-office companionship for Ken. And me? I relished his openness, not to mention his appreciation of my cooking. Sometimes his visit was the highlight of my week.

One Sunday when Ken stepped out of the room, I poured out the story of our troubled marriage. "Ken won't communicate with me!" I wailed. "He won't give of himself!" I lowered my voice so Steven and Tim wouldn't hear. "We're considering separation. In fact, Ken's slept at the office the last few nights."

Hall's forehead wrinkled in distress. "Oh no, Shirley! You can't let your family break up! No! No! No!"

Right then and there he bowed his head, folded his rough hands, and prayed for us. "Dear Jesus, please help my good friends Ken and Shirley and the boys. And please show me how to help them too. Amen." Then he turned to me. "I'll pray for you every day, Shirley," he promised.

I thanked him, but I doubted he'd remember. His memory was so poor! Anyway, I didn't see how such simple, childlike prayers could help with our complicated problems.

Hall surprised me. He remembered, he prayed, and a couple of weeks later he told me he'd received an answer. "The Lord showed me where you and Ken should begin," he insisted.

The minute I'd finished the dinner dishes, Hall made Ken and me sit down at the kitchen table. He took two sheets of paper from his pocket, found a couple of pencils, and shoved them toward us. "Shirley," he said sternly, "write down five things you like about Ken."

He turned to Ken. "Ken, you write five things you like about Shirley."

Ken and I looked at each other in embarrassment. "Oh, Hall, no! This is ridiculous!"

"Write!" he ordered, folding his arms and glaring at us.

Five things? I couldn't even think of one. I glanced at Ken. His pencil, too, was poised above still-blank paper. Then I noticed his arms—those strong, hairy arms that had attracted me to Ken in the first place. I still liked them, so I wrote: #1. Strong, hairy arms.

I thought awhile longer. Ken wasn't only strong, he was also gentle: #2. He's gentle. And Ken was patient: #3. He's patient. Whew! Three down, only two to go. Well... #4. He's kind. #5. He's rarely critical.

I assumed Hall was going to pray about our lists. I assumed wrong. "Now you must read your lists to each other," he instructed.

. What a revelation! It had been years since I'd told Ken how much I liked his arms. He'd never told me he appreciated my cooking and housekeeping skills. I'd never said, "Thank you, Ken, for being patient and kind." He'd never said, "I like your honesty and perceptiveness."

Suddenly Hall's silly little exercise didn't seem quite so silly.

Over the next few weeks, Hall made us delve into our backgrounds. We discovered that my family had been emotional, even explosive, while Ken's had been reserved. Under Hall's guidance we discussed our expectations of marriage—spiritual, financial, and physical. We listed traits and habits we wanted the other person to change. We admitted our own shortcomings to each other. Later, when we sought further counseling, we discovered that Hall's methods had been similar to the ones many professionals use to help couples communicate better. But Hall's ideas had come to him through prayer and the inspiration of the Holy Spirit.

Our marriage improved, but I still felt a nagging sense of emptiness. The secret of real love still eluded me. Jesus knew it. Hall knew it. Would I? Ever?

I didn't have much time to dwell on it, though, because Hall's condition began deteriorating. He'd lived an incredible eight years since the tumor had been discovered. Now it was growing again—rapidly—and nothing could halt it.

Twice, tragic fires consumed Hall's homes and his worldly goods. Eventually he was taken to the nursing home where he had visited patients so many times. His mind was nearly gone, his body so wasted he could barely lift his head from the pillow. Yet he still could love. That was obvious from the glow on his face when someone mentioned Jesus.

Hall died, but his funeral was a celebration of victory. Hall had not only triumphed over incredibly adverse circumstances, but he had touched hundreds of people with God's love. The flower-filled church overflowed with those people—black and white, rich and poor, elderly and young.

As the organ signaled the end of the service, I looked past the casket to Ken. We'd both miss Hall, I knew, yet we were glad his ordeal was over. Now he was at home with the Lord, whole and free. As I thought about that, I smiled through my tears. Ken smiled back.

Slowly, in my mind, something registered. I smiled...Ken smiled back. I gave...Ken responded.

That moment—that simple exchange of smiles—stayed with me. I began to understand what Hall had shown me by his own example. To experience love, I had only to give it. I had wanted to be wrapped in a great sense of Ken's love for me, but I had been too wrapped up in myself to seek that love in positive ways. I thanked God that I could change that. I would start loving Ken tonight—by cooking his favorite meal. I'd zipper my mouth if he was late coming home to dinner. And maybe tomorrow I could begin his day with a big hug and some words of encouragement.

I took a deep breath. At last I knew the secret of love, and it wasn't a secret at all. It was written in one of my favorite Bible verses. "Beloved, let us love one another, for love is of God" (1 John 4:7 ESV).

Hall had said the same thing on his first Sunday visit. "I can still love! And that's the most important thing there is."

Love Never Fails

Love...always protects, always trusts,
always hopes, always perseveres. Love never fails....
These three remain: faith, hope and love
But the greatest of these is love.

1 CORINTHIANS 13:6–8, 13 NIV

Saving Mount Vernon

BY THOMAS FLEMING

The year was 1853, and Ann Pamela Cunningham faced an uncertain future. Ann was thirty-seven years old and disabled. Born on her family's plantation near Waterloo, South Carolina, she had attended Barhamville, one of the best women's schools in the South. Her intelligence impressed everyone. She expected to lead a quiet, cultured life, but shortly after her graduation she was thrown from a horse and suffered severe spinal injuries. The life she'd envisioned for herself was not to be. More than once she wondered why God had sent her into this world to leave her almost helpless.

Each year her devoted mother took her to Philadelphia, at that time the center of American medicine. Over the course of several months she underwent the latest treatments for her condition, but doctors never gave her much hope of improvement. In the fall of 1853, after her mother left her in Philadelphia for more treatments, Ann Pamela felt especially sad and lonely.

Soon she received a letter from her mother. Mrs. Cunningham wrote about how she had traveled by steamboat down the Potomac River. The first evening she heard the ship's bell because the boat was passing Mount Vernon, George Washington's home. Steamboat captains often showed this mark of respect.

Mrs. Cunningham had gone on deck. A full moon illuminated the landscape. When Washington was still alive, Mrs. Cunningham had visited Mount Vernon. She remembered the impressive white house and the vast lawns. Now she saw nothing but decay. The wharf sagged and bare patches disfigured the lawn.

"I was painfully distressed at the ruin and desolation," she wrote her daughter. "The thought passed through my mind: Why was it that the women of Washington's country did not try to keep it in repair, if the men could not do it?"

In her Philadelphia room Ann Pamela read and reread that letter. *I will do it!* she vowed, her mind suddenly ablaze with determination. I will save Mount Vernon! From that moment until her death twenty-two years later, she never wavered in her conviction that God had given her this unique task.

The following morning a visitor found her writing a public letter to the women of the South, urging them to join her in this tremendous undertaking. Published in the *Charleston Mercury* on December 2, 1853, the missive was signed anonymously, "A Southern Matron."

In those days women were not supposed to have any kind of public role. Ann Pamela was hesitant to violate this tradition, but she soon realized she would have to take the risk. As many women responded to her appeal, she took it upon herself to write the owner of Mount Vernon, John Augustine Washington, Jr., the great-grandnephew of the founder, asking him if he would sell the estate.

Ann received a chilly reply. Washington wanted to sell Mount Vernon only to the state of Virginia or the federal government. No one else, he assumed, would be able to meet his asking price of $200,000. In an era when a laborer was paid a dollar a day, how could a group of women hope to raise such an amount? Ann Pamela had faith that God would help her find a way.

In Boston, the popular orator and statesman Edward Everett heard about her campaign. Intrigued, he went to Philadelphia to meet her. His own career had been on the wane because of failing health, but he had given a lecture on Washington that won him local acclaim. At first he was not impressed with Ann Pamela. "An invalid maiden lady seems the last person to manage a difficult business affair," he wrote in his journal. But by the time he left Philadelphia, he had committed all the proceeds of future Washington lectures to the crusade.

Everett's health improved, and over the next three years he gave his Washington lecture 129 times.

Ann Pamela was campaigning on two other fronts. She organized her volunteers into the Mount Vernon Ladies' Association, with herself as regent, and she appointed a vice regent for each state in the South. She managed to convince the Virginia state legislature to grant a charter to the organization. Then she went to work persuading the owner of Mount Vernon to take them seriously.

Ignoring pain and fatigue, Ann Pamela journeyed to Mount Vernon in June 1856. She became so absorbed in an intense discussion with John Augustine Washington, Jr., and his wife that she missed her steamboat home. She boarded a sailboat and was towed into midstream to meet another boat but missed that too. Returning to the Mount Vernon wharf, she was too exhausted to travel farther. But at that moment, realizing she would have to spend the night at the mansion, she felt an inner confidence. God had brought her this close. *Mount Vernon will be ours,* she thought.

Ann stayed in her room that afternoon and evening, gathering her strength. Then after supper she was carried downstairs to the parlor, where the discussion continued. That night she won Mrs. Washington to her cause.

The following morning she reopened the argument with John Augustine. "The spirit moved me as it never had before," she said later.

Ann dazzled John Augustine with the names of distinguished Southern women who had joined the association. Adding a touch of humor, she pointed out that it was a leap year, which meant a woman should get her way. Finally, as he helped her into a waiting carriage, she held out her hand. "With quivering lips, moist eyes, and a heart too full for him to speak," she wrote, "our compact was closed in silence."

Her work was by no means done. John Augustine set a deadline of spring 1858 for the association to raise a down payment of $18,000, with the balance to be paid in four annual installments. Ann Pamela agreed to those terms, though at the time of the signing she was so ill someone had to hold her hand and guide the pen.

Ann set a more difficult deadline for herself and the Mount Vernon Ladies' Association. They were going to raise the balance due in ten months! She wanted to take advantage of the publicity the sale had won for them, and she was keenly aware a civil war was looming.

So far most of the money had been raised in the South. It was time to tap the resources of the North. Swiftly, Ann Pamela appointed vice regents for the northern states. One of them was New Yorker Mary Morris Hamilton, granddaughter of Alexander Hamilton. With energy worthy of her famous ancestor, Miss Hamilton soon had deputies raising funds in every county of the Empire State.

Edward Everett redoubled his oratorical efforts and took on the added task of writing a weekly newspaper column on George Washington, donating the payment to the association. He raised a staggering $69,000. The famed actor Edwin Booth donated the proceeds from one of his performances. Washington Irving, the country's best-known writer, gave $500. A chess champion named Paul Murphy played four opponents while blindfolded, beat them, and raised $300. Even the newsboys of New York City gave their pennies.

By December 1858 the Mount Vernon Ladies' Association paid the first installment of $57,000 to John Augustine

Washington, Jr., three months before it was due. On George Washington's birthday in 1859, they paid another installment. By mid-December that year, Regent Cunningham proudly announced that Mount Vernon was now "the property of the nation."

The timing could not have been more providential. In October of 1859, John Brown had seized the federal arsenal at Harper's Ferry, hoping to arm Virginia's slaves. The incident sharply accelerated the slide toward secession and civil war. When the tragic conflict began, the Ladies' Association persuaded both sides to declare Mount Vernon a neutral zone.

When peace returned in 1865, Ann Pamela launched a fund-raising campaign to restore Mount Vernon and Washington's tomb with exacting authenticity. She set a standard that has made her a guiding force of the historical preservation movement in America. By the time she died in 1875, Mount Vernon had become what this amazing woman had envisioned—"a bond of Union that will never be eradicated." Today Ann Pamela Cunningham stands as her own monument to the idea that personal faith and unwavering determination can achieve the impossible.

Unwavering Faith

Face your deficiencies and acknowledge them....
Let them teach you patience, sweetness, insight. When
we do the best we can, we never know what miracle is
wrought in our life, or in the life of another....
I thank God for my handicaps, for through them
I have found myself, my work, and my God.

HELEN KELLER

Not My Plan

BY TRISHA DAY GERCKEN

By the time Joe and I decided it was time to start a family, I had it planned down to the last detail. I shopped for cribs, interviewed obstetricians, and painted the spare room pink. I even had an entire scenario worked out for the happy day when I would surprise Joe with the announcement of my pregnancy. I would make a huge bouquet of pink and blue balloons and tie it to the garage door. Joe would pull up in his car, eyes full of questions. Then I would present him with a lighthearted poem I had composed, and he would scoop me up in his arms.

There was only one hitch: months passed and I didn't conceive. One bleak evening, I could no longer hide my disappointment. "Joe, I'm so sorry," I said, bursting into tears. "I want us to have a family so badly."

Joe hugged me. "Trisha, it's all right," he said soothingly. "We're already a family."

That made me cry harder. Joe was wonderful with our nieces and nephews, and now he'd never be able to read bedtime stories to our own child. I felt overwhelmed with guilt and despair. "Lord, please help me," I prayed. "All I've ever wanted is to be a mother."

I became even more determined. Morning after morning for the next year, I followed the advice in several books on infertility, sticking a thermometer in my mouth, charting my hormonal changes, and tracking the times when I was supposed to be most fertile. But my efforts went unrewarded, and my frustration mounted.

One day after lunch as I was hurrying back to the office, I got stuck behind a woman in a station wagon. I stared at the car and noticed a bumper sticker proclaiming, "My child is an honor roll student." Three little blond heads were visible in the backseat. *It's not fair*, I thought. *Why does she have three kids when I can't even have one?*

Joe and I had started attending a new church around the time we decided to have a child, and I didn't have the quiet assurance Joe's faith seemed to give him. One morning he actually announced, "Trisha, I've been thanking God for the baby he's going to send us."

Hoping I could gain the same sort of confidence, I began reading the Bible carefully, looking for some comfort in its pages. But as the months went by and I didn't become pregnant, I was nagged by terrible doubts. *The Bible says children are a blessing,* I thought. *Well, if I'm not receiving that blessing, then somehow I must not be worthy.*

Finally, I became so filled with despair I made an appointment with our pastor to ask him for help. "What have I done wrong? Why am I being punished?" I cried. "Why can't I get pregnant?"

"Trisha," Pastor John answered gently, "God's not punishing you. He wants you to have the desires of your heart. Do you want a boy or a girl?"

"A girl," I whispered hesitantly.

Pastor John held my hand as we prayed together for a baby girl. When I left church, I felt more encouraged than I had in a long time. The next week, I happened to tune in to a radio program in the middle of a discussion on infertility. "If you're looking for professional help," one panelist advised, "then run, don't walk, to a reproductive endocrinologist." That was something I hadn't heard of, much less tried, before. I rushed to the phone book and found a listing for a Dr. Kevin Winslow.

In August, Joe and I sat down and talked with Dr. Winslow for more than an hour. He went over our fears and anxieties as well as our medical histories. "What's your timetable?" he asked. "A year? Two years?"

"Yesterday," I replied, only half joking.

"Infertility is a long, hard battle," Dr. Winslow said. "One you'll have to be prepared for emotionally."

After testing, Joe was declared healthy. I, on the other hand, had to have major surgery to remove scar tissue (from a childhood appendectomy) that obstructed my reproductive organs. It all seemed worth it, though, when I had the first signs of pregnancy in December. As I sat in Dr. Winslow's office eagerly awaiting the test results, I envisioned a wonderful Christmas scene. Three generations of my family would be gathered at my parents' house on the Gulf Coast. As the lights from the tree sparkled, I would announce the news of my pregnancy. Mom would be so happy she'd—

Dr. Winslow interrupted my daydream. "I'm sorry, Trisha," he said. "The test was negative."

Not pregnant even after everything I've done, after all I've gone through?

Dr. Winslow tried to comfort me, but I was inconsolable. I stumbled into the parking garage. "Aren't You hearing anything I'm asking?" I yelled at God as I headed to my car.

Somehow I made it through the holidays, but my dissatisfaction threatened to overwhelm me. Then one February morning, I was struck with abdominal pain so fierce that I sped to Dr. Winslow's.

As he began the examination, I wondered what more could possibly happen in my attempts to become pregnant. I strained to see the ultrasound monitor, but nothing showed up except scratchy shadow. Then a white speck like a tiny star rolled into view. Dr. Winslow continued moving the probe. At that moment a strange certainty seized me: *that's my baby!*

My mind was spinning with such emotion that I heard only fragments of what Dr. Winslow was telling me. "There's a mass on your right ovary, but there is a pregnancy situation...possibly a threatened miscarriage...no heartbeat yet..."

Finally I was hearing the words I had dreamed of, even if my baby was in trouble. As soon as I got home I dialed Joe's office. The words tumbled out almost faster than I could say them. "I went to the doctor and saw a spot. There's no heartbeat, and I'm bleeding. But it's a baby, Joe, it's a baby!"

Several days later Joe took me for a second ultrasound. First the ominous white blob came into view. There was darkness for a few seconds when at once a luminous star appeared. It was flashing, pulsing rapidly like a bird's fluttering wing—our baby's heartbeat!

Joe's shoulders rolled and he started laughing. At first I leaned over to hush him, but soon I was laughing too, overcome with joy. The horrible days of uncertainty and frustration were behind us. I was on my way to motherhood!

I outfitted myself with a complete wardrobe of maternity clothes. For one giddy, happy week I waltzed through life wearing an enormous tent of a jumper and a huge smile.

Then one day I awoke in horrible pain. Joe had already left for work, so my neighbors drove me to the hospital. An efficient nurse hooked me up to an IV. "If you're having a miscarriage, you're going to need blood," she said crisply. I stiffened at her careless words.

I was wheeled to the ultrasound room, and a technician began the familiar examination. The phone rang. "No, sir," I heard him say. "There's no fetal activity at all. No sign of life."

No sign of life? I cried as I have never cried in my life. I was wheeled into another room where nurses kept fussing over me with more procedures. I wanted them to leave me alone so I could scream until my ears hurt.

Pastor John tiptoed in. At first, he just gently rubbed my arm. I knew he was trying to be kind, but I couldn't respond. Finally he asked, "Trisha, do you feel the presence of God?"

It was more than I could handle.

"No!" I cried. I wanted to spew out, "My baby's dead! How can God be here when all I've ever wanted is gone?" It took my last shred of mental energy to stay calm.

Pastor John bowed his head. "God, please comfort Trisha," he prayed. "Her pain is making it hard for her to reach out to You. Let her know You're here."

I sobbed bitterly as he left. An hour later the ultrasound technician poked his head in. "The doctor has ordered another scan."

My friend Darla, who had just arrived, brandished her soda can at him and announced, "I'm going with her."

I was plunged back into the ultrasound room, that dreaded place where my baby had been pronounced dead. Darla leaned against a small metal table next to my IV pole. The monitor hummed in the darkness as the technician maneuvered the probe.

Suddenly Darla leaped up, spilling her soda and knocking over the table. The IV needle jerked out of my wrist, but I barely felt it. There on the screen was a flickering dot. A heartbeat! My baby was alive!

I started laughing and crying at the same time. "Twins!" the dumbfounded technician exclaimed. "Here's the empty amniotic sac where you miscarried one of them."

It was bittersweet news. I felt a pang of sorrow for the baby I had lost. But I was overjoyed about the baby I still carried. I stared at the tiny pulsing light, transfixed. "Thank You, Lord!" Darla exulted.

Her words penetrated my daze. Suddenly I understood. My prayers—and Joe's and Pastor John's—had been answered through a scenario I could never have imagined. I could hope and plan all I wanted, but it wasn't my timetable that mattered—it was God's. His love couldn't be measured by whether things went according to some script I had mapped out. *O Lord*, I thought, *thank You for my baby. And for always listening, even when I didn't realize it.*

The roller-coaster ride of my pregnancy continued, but I never again felt alone. Not when I had radical surgery to remove a tumor growing around my uterus. Not when I developed mild toxemia. Not when I found out I had gestational diabetes.

In October, our beautiful, healthy baby girl arrived. She had Joe's huge blue eyes and the plumpest, rosiest cheeks I'd ever seen. We chose her name carefully. Erica means "powerful," and Faith stands for belief and trust in God. Erica Faith is a constant reminder to me that all I need is a strong faith. God's plan will take care of the rest.

Powerful Trust

Trust in the Lord with all your heart
And do not lean on your own understanding.
In all your ways acknowledge Him,
And He will make your paths straight.

PROVERBS 3:5–6 NASB

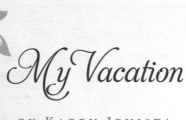

My Vacation

Pete took me fishing on one of our first dates. We were living in southern California back then, and it was a good way for us to spend time alone really getting to know each other. Maybe I didn't share his passion for fishing, or even quite understand it, but I loved his straightforwardness. He saw me as capable and steady; I loved his sense of adventure;.

At our June wedding, we vowed to work hard at making ours a partnership that thrived.

Eventually our jobs, a newborn baby, and the responsibilities of everyday life limited Pete's time with rod and reel. Then he and his friend Jeff came up with a plan: They'd drive deep into Baja California and spend several days camping and fishing in Mexico's Sea of Cortés. Laughing at these two overgrown Boy Scouts, I gave my blessing. From then on, Friday nights they spent hours on the phone, going over maps and fantasizing about catching the prized dorado—a powerful game fish with golden scales and blue fins. "A fisherman's dream," Pete claimed.

Shortly after our third wedding anniversary, my husband took his first vacation without me. He came home with fish to

64

last us months and a smile that didn't leave his face for almost as long.

Before I knew it, the trip had become an annual tradition. Each year it seemed to wear on me a little more. Come spring, Pete and Jeff started planning—and Pete and I started arguing. I worried about the guys. I'd seen their pictures of their "vacation spot," a remote Mexican beach six hundred miles from the US border, where the heat and humidity were brutal and a phone was as rare as a cool breeze. They fished out of an inflatable boat to which they'd attached an outboard motor. How safe was that?

But I was also resentful. Pete's fishing buddy was single. Was Pete wishing he was too and taking a vacation from me? To make matters worse, our move north to Oregon lengthened the drive to Baja, leaving me home alone with two children for ten days.

Otherwise our relationship was healthy, and we got involved leading couples' retreats for our church. During weekend get-aways, we gave practical advice on working out the sticky issues of a marriage. Pete and I never used the fishing trip as an example, but on one of those weekends I confided in a friend. "I know Pete. He'd stop going if I asked, but I wish he'd give it up all on his own."

"Why don't you go with him?" my friend suggested.

"What mom can pick up and disappear for ten days?" I shot back. "And if I could, I sure wouldn't spend them in a fishing boat!" Not that Pete wanted me tagging along on his macho adventure, anyway.

We were in a rut. Then one night Pete sat down at the kitchen counter with his tackle box while I read the paper. When he said something about "our ten-year anniversary," I was confused.

"We were married in '86, Pete," I said. "It'll be thirteen years."

"I meant the fishing trips, Karen. This will be number ten!"

I put down the paper. "I'll never understand it," I muttered, getting up.

"Honey," Pete said, sounding tired, "we can't keep fighting about this. Do you want me to cancel? Please just tell me." He waited for my answer.

"How about this year I go with you guys," I said, smirking.

"I never dreamed...," he started to say. *Gotcha, Pete!* Then he hopped off the counter stool. "Great!" he whooped, grabbing me in a bear hug. "The water, the sunsets, the local people—and the fish, man, the fish! I can't wait to show you. Thank you, Karen. Thank you." He kissed me. "I'll call Jeff."

Hold on a minute, I thought, panicking. *What just happened here?*

There was no turning back. Over the next few months, Pete reworked the plans. He knew I couldn't do any kind of camping that didn't include toilets, so the guys picked a new fishing spot near a small motel and agreed to stay there. Pete lined up his mom to watch the kids, and we switched the trip to September, when they were in school. As our departure day drew near, Pete's excitement built in proportion to my apprehension.

I prayed as we pulled out of the driveway to begin the three-day drive to Baja, *God, please use this trip to make a real and lasting change in my marriage.*

On the way to California, where we'd pick up Jeff, Pete gave me a few pointers on dorado. "If you hook one, I can guarantee it's gonna jump, and that fish is strong enough to break a line. You have to use a gaff hook to get it in the boat. It's not an easy catch. But the real bonus is, the fish tastes as good as it looks."

Jeff took over at the wheel when he joined us in Fresno, and on day three, after a sixteen-hour stretch of driving, we arrived at our motel in Mulegé. We unloaded only to pile back into the truck and start to head off-road to the beach to catch our dinner.

"In the dark?" I said. "You guys don't waste a minute."

On the way, though, we punctured a tire and Pete broke the lug wrench trying to unbolt the spare. We hiked a mile to the main highway and hitched back to the motel. The guys got their spare wrench and returned to the truck. I collapsed in the room, with barely enough energy to brush my teeth with bottled water. This was a vacation?

The next morning after breakfast, we prepared for a day of fishing. I was impressed with the guys' organization—board and knives for skinning, boning, and filleting the day's catch, baggies and cooler at the ready. We fished a beautiful reef about five miles offshore. They reeled in sea bass and snapper. I watched my husband, completely at home in this environment where, to him, labor and relaxation were the same thing.

The wind kicked up about noon, and the guys cranked the motor. "We have to get in fast," they explained. "This boat isn't made for windy weather."

We covered the distance at top speed, bouncing wildly across white-capped swells. I cowered, keeping a death grip on the side handles. At the boat ramp, I staggered weak-kneed to the truck and fell across the seat. *What am I doing here, Lord?*

Something brushed against my ankle, and I looked down. A bug the size of a catfish was crawling up my calf. I exploded out of the truck, swatting at the huge beetle until it dropped into the dirt.

I caught my breath and rejoined the guys, who were filleting fish on the beach. We had a picnic lunch then fished offshore the rest of the day. Back at the motel, we grilled our dinner outside. Pete and I sat quietly, holding hands and watching the sun set behind the desert. I remembered dates early on, when our silence meant I love you. Pete squeezed my hand as if thinking the same thing.

There was much discussion the next morning about hooking dorado. After polling the locals, we settled on a fishing spot. Finally Jeff pulled in a small one. The guys got their hopes up and switched to using squid for bait. Then I felt a tug on my line. Some kind of golden fish flashed in the distance just beneath the surface of the water. "Hey, guys," I said, "check this out." Pete quickly turned and looked.

"Doraaa-do!" he yelled. "And it's a beaut!" The fish must have jumped seven feet out of the water, the sun brightening its blue fins like stained glass.

Pete took charge. "Don't reel while he's running, Karen!" Jeff handed Pete the gaff while I held the rod for dear life. "Give him some line," Pete said. "When he stops to rest, reel.... Now hold steady." For fifteen minutes we worked together to get the big fish into the boat.

Jeff shouted when we finally won the battle. "What a catch!"

Pete broke out the scale. "Twelve pounds," he said. Then he stood up and yelled at the top of his lungs, "My wife caught a big fish, baby—yeah!" He pumped his fist and shook me by my shoulders, bursting with pride. "Good job, Karen," he said, his hold on me turning tender. I looked deep into his eyes.

"So this is why you come," I said, understanding just a little more deeply this man I'd spent thirteen years getting to know. The last few days, I'd watched him doing something he loved and for one brief moment I loved it too. But what I loved most was my husband's wanting to share what he loved with me.

"There are more dorado out there," Pete said, baiting another hook. But I'd gotten what I came for.

I've stopped calling Pete's annual fishing trip a vacation. It's a quest, really, for dorado, for camaraderie, and for victory over hardship. The year I went, I was on a quest for the perfect marriage. And I came close, as close as I could, to understanding Pete completely. Then God filled in the gap. With a twelve-pound dorado, He showed me that I'd made more than one great catch in my life.

Grow in Love

A long-term marriage has to move beyond chemistry
to compatibility, to friendship, to companionship.
It is certainly not that passion disappears,
but that it is conjoined with other ways of love.

MADELEINE L'ENGLE

The Visitor

BY REBECCA BATESON

Like most mothers, I've watched my share of hospital dramas on T.V. A child rolled into the ER on a gurney. The frantic staff. The life-and-death tension. *What if that were my Andrew?* I'd wonder.

I'd never been super religious, but I'd always felt I had a deal with God: I'd never ask for lots of money or a big house, and I'd always thank Him for what He did give me. In return, all I wanted was for Him to keep things on an even keel. *Just don't give me more than I can handle*, I'd pray.

Then one terrible night, the six-year-old on the gurney was my little boy. He was rushed to Hasbro Children's Hospital in Providence, Rhode Island, fighting meningococcemia, a deadly form of meningitis. All at once it felt as if my deal with God were off the table.

Andrew was such a normal kid—frisky, athletic, the type of boy who wolfed down his lunch, itching to get back outside and play. The evening he got sick, he'd been running around outside with his sister and cousins. Later, we went for ice cream. That's when it happened.

"Mom, my legs hurt," he said. "I feel so tired."

I felt his forehead. It was burning up. By the time we got home, he was shivering, with a 102-degree fever.

"Probably the flu," I told Scott, my husband, and put Andrew to bed. I hoped it was just a twenty-four-hour bug. The next day was the Fourth of July, and we had a big family picnic planned. But that night he threw up several times. By morning his face had taken on a grayish pallor. He was limp and didn't feel like doing anything. I called our family doctor. He recommended we take him to the hospital for tests.

By the time we arrived at the hospital, red, pinprick-like dots had spread across his body. Hemorrhages. The ER nurse had seen these symptoms before.

"We're going to take him to the trauma room," the nurse said. Within minutes, the pinpricks had grown to purple splotches on his stomach, thighs, and neck. The chief physician pulled us aside while the ER team pumped Andrew full of antibiotics.

"We're pretty sure your son has meningitis," he said. "The antibiotics have probably killed the bacteria by now."

"So he's going to be okay?" Scott asked.

The doctor shook his head. "We got the bacteria but not before it sent millions of toxins into Andrew's system. He's probably going to get sicker."

A chill went through me. Bacterial meningitis is one of the most aggressive illnesses known to man. Scott and I stared at Andrew. Our son was changing before our eyes. The emergency staff couldn't stop the hemorrhaging. Andrew's whole body grew puffy. Much of his skin turned almost blackish, as if from severe burns.

"Scott," I said, trying to hold back tears, "he doesn't even look like our son anymore."

We turned to the doctor for some positive sign. He didn't give one. Only later would we learn that the mortality rate for a case this severe approached 80 percent. Gently, the doctor said, "You need to prepare yourselves. I can't predict whether or not Andrew will survive."

Andrew was moved to the ICU. We stayed up that night watching him. He was hooked to so many tubes, he looked more like a lab rat than our boy. *You've got to fight, Andrew,* I thought. *You've got to fight hard.* I closed my eyes. *Lord, I prayed, I don't know how much more I can take. I don't know if I can handle this. I thought we had a deal.*

Yet Andrew did not improve. Each day brought a new crisis. Andrew's kidneys failed. He needed to be put on a ventilator. Finally, the doctors induced a coma to relieve his pain. Andrew's hands turned cold, then curled into frozen claws. The hemorrhaging had virtually cut off circulation to his extremities. His toes and legs were literally dying.

A week after Andrew entered the hospital, one of his doctors asked to talk to us. She led us to a consultation room down the hall from Andrew's room. "Andrew's blood vessels are blocked to the point where they may be ruined," she said. "Once that happens, it's hard to reestablish circulation. There's a good chance we're going to have to amputate."

I held it together till the doctor left. I expected to break down. Instead, I flushed with anger. God wasn't keeping His part of the bargain. My boy might lose his hands and legs. He might die. *Why are You doing this to a child?* I asked bitterly. *Why are You doing this to our family?*

Nothing changed, no matter how angry I got. In Andrew's second week in the hospital, with his legs an awful purple-black, the doctors ordered a bone scan. Three hours later, the results came in.

"There's nothing. No circulation at all below the knees," the orthopedist said. "We have to amputate his legs. If we don't, it could jeopardize his life."

I couldn't speak. I tried to picture Andrew—my active little boy—in a wheelchair. A wheelchair!

Following the operation, Andrew remained in a coma for days. All I could do was sit there and watch him, my heart filled with sorrow and bitterness. But that burden was nothing compared to the time I knew was coming—when Andrew would awaken and we'd have to tell him about his legs. If he awakened.

He did. He finally turned the corner. Scott and I walked into his hospital room. Andrew was watching TV. "Honey," I said, "we really need to talk about what happened to you." Scott and I stood on either side of his bed. "You were very sick. You're getting better, but your legs didn't get better so the doctors had to take them off. If they didn't, hon, you wouldn't have gotten better. But we're going to get you new legs."

Andrew started to cry. "I want my old legs back," he repeated again and again, between sobs.

I wanted to cry too. But I couldn't in front of him. All I could do was hold Andrew and say, "You can't have them. They won't work anymore." And wonder again, *Lord, how could You do this to a child? I'm at my breaking point. Can't You see?*

I was still fighting to keep from crying when Andrew asked a new question. "Mom, will I ever be able to walk again?"

"Oh yeah," I told him. "I've heard of kids who've done all kinds of things."

"Will I be able to run?"

"It's going to take some work, but I don't see why not."

"How will I ride my bike?"

"We'll figure it out," I said.

Andrew fell asleep, but I couldn't. *Lord, won't You finally help us?* I asked.

At last, in early September, Andrew was well enough to come home. I was relieved and also worried sick. How would Andrew hold up emotionally when he saw how different life without legs would be?

It was tough. Andrew had been fitted with prosthetics right before he came home. It's one thing to have one artificial leg. At least you can balance on the other, feel where you're going. But two legs! Rehab was incredibly hard—and slow. The doctors warned us that Andrew probably wouldn't take his first unassisted steps till November—if then.

I could see the frustration in his face when kids would zip past our house on their bicycles. As for myself, I was just worn out. I used to pray in anger at God. Now I didn't even have the energy to do that. I wasn't even sure where God was anymore. I felt abandoned, and it was worse, far worse than feeling simply angry. This was a cold, dark space in my heart, as if my faith had been taken away like my son's legs.

Then one night at the dinner table, Andrew said out of nowhere, "I saw God, Mommy. I was sleeping at the hospital. He put His arms out, and I thought He was going to give me a hug. But instead He just touched me on the shoulder."

"Did He say anything?" I asked.

"No, He was just...there."

A chill ran down my spine. *He was just there.* What did that mean? I looked at Andrew, wolfing down his dinner. For months all I'd seen was a handicapped child, a damaged child, fighting as hard as he could, failing more often than succeeding in his rehab. Falling down, unable to master his new legs. Yet, unlike me, he'd never turned bitter, never given up. "I'm going to walk, and I'm going to ride my bike," he'd insist. "You just watch."

Andrew has come through this better than I have. He was moving on. But I was stuck in my bitterness and sense of spiritual betrayal. *He was just there.* Had God been there all along for me too, and I was too angry to see? Was He there for me now? *Lord, thank You for being with Andrew. Be with me now too.*

Andrew had been in therapy for a while, and three weeks before he'd managed a few cautious steps—but only with the support of parallel bars. Then one day in October, the family was sitting in the living room. Suddenly, with no warning, Andrew struggled to his feet. Without a word he walked slowly, awkwardly, across the living room on his own. And then back again. "Did you see that?" Scott asked. I was dumbstruck. The doctors had predicted he wouldn't walk before Christmas. My eyes filled with tears. But in my mind's eye, clear and unwavering, I saw my boy walking again with a strong hand on his shoulder. He was just there.

Andrew is fifteen now. He rides his bike, he plays basketball, and he's even on a hockey team. Sometimes when I'm at one of his games, I'll see him fall and I'll think, *Andrew, you shouldn't be doing this. It's too much.* But then I catch myself. I hear a voice whisper, *"Don't be afraid. I'm here. I can handle that."*

He Is Here

God is our refuge and strength,
an ever-present help in trouble.
Therefore we will not fear, though the earth give way
and the mountains fall into the heart of the sea,
though its waters roar and foam
and the mountains quake with their surging....
The LORD Almighty is with us.

PSALM 46:1–3, 7 NIV

A Perfect Match

A t the first of the year, I put up my new calendar in the kitchen, feeling like I'd finally gotten my life back on track. The past year since my divorce had been a long, hard struggle, but my three boys and I had adjusted to our single-mom household. My job at a furniture factory kept food on the table and paid the bills. And I'd started going to church again with my mom. I couldn't quite believe as she did that God had a deep, personal interest in our lives—I figured He had more important things to worry about than me—but I definitely found comfort in being closer to Him.

One morning toward the end of January I saw the boys onto the school bus and was about to leave for my shift when the phone rang. "I'm from the Red Cross," the caller said. "I got your name from a bone-marrow donor registry."

Donor registry? Then I remembered. Two years earlier I'd seen a picture of a baby in the newspaper. Something in his big blue eyes called out to me, so I read the article. The baby needed a bone-marrow transplant, and the story pleaded for people to go to the Red Cross and take a simple blood test to see if their marrow could save the baby's life.

Back then things had just about hit rock bottom for me. My marriage was falling apart, and I worried what it was doing to the kids. I'd had to watch my dream of finding work where I could really see myself helping people, like physical therapy, get swallowed up by the grind of the factory job I'd taken to make ends meet.

Well, maybe even a failure like me can help someone, I had thought. So I'd gotten tested. Although I hadn't been a match for the baby, I felt better having at least tried to do something for someone else. But with my husband and me going our separate ways and all the stress of starting over on my own, I forgot about the donor list until the person from the Red Cross called that morning.

"There's a chance that you're a match for a twenty-four-year-old woman with leukemia," she said. "Could you come in for another blood test? If you're still willing to become a donor, that is."

"I'd like to try," I replied slowly, that old longing to do something for someone else stirring in me. I'd been blessed with good health my whole life. Maybe this was my time to share it.

I turned out to be an almost perfect match for the woman with leukemia. "Only an identical twin," a doctor informed me, "could be a better donor." I looked over the booklet on bone-marrow transplants. Even though the picture of the equipment used in the procedure made me shudder—I didn't know they made needles that long!—there wasn't any question in my mind that I'd go through with it.

My kids were too young to understand what a bone marrow transplant involved, but my mom was afraid something might go wrong. "I'm putting your name on the prayer chain at church," she insisted. I wasn't real big on prayer, but I figured it couldn't hurt.

On March 10, I went to the transplant center just across the state line in Minneapolis. I was so nervous that the doctors teased me about how badly my hands were shaking. But before I knew it the procedure was over, and the marrow extracted from my pelvic bones was on its way to that twenty-four-year-old woman, waiting at another hospital somewhere in the United States.

Except for some soreness that went away pretty quickly, I didn't have any aftereffects from the procedure. I couldn't stop thinking about it, though, wondering how the woman who'd received the marrow was doing. By law we weren't allowed to know each other's identities until a year after the transplant, so all I had to go by were the regular updates from the Red Cross. They said she was suffering complications: double vision, unexplained fevers, graft-versus-host disease.

It worried me enough that I asked Mom to add the woman to the prayer chain. In September the Red Cross told me that the recipient was home from the hospital. It looked like the transplant had worked!

Things in my own life took an upswing after that. Around Christmas I started dating Randy Bertrand, a friend of mine from the factory. I liked how he gave me a smile whenever he drove the forklift by my workstation and stuck around to help me finish my work when my neck was aching one day. He was the kind of guy I could count on.

On the one-year anniversary of the transplant, the Red Cross sent me a letter with the recipient's name and address: Rhonda Dietze, Medford, Wisconsin—only seventy-five miles away! Pretty soon we were trading letters, photos, and phone calls.

"I don't know what to say," Rhonda confessed the first time we talked. "'Thank you' doesn't seem like enough, considering what you've done for me."

"Well, I have to admit, helping you made me feel better too," I said. "I'm just glad everything worked out."

"So am I." Rhonda sounded like she looked in her pictures— gentle, unassuming, and sweet-natured. I thought Randy and I were quiet, but she was even more shy than we were. Though I really wanted to meet her in person and see for myself that she was doing all right, I decided to wait until she brought it up.

In the meantime we got to know each other long-distance. It was uncanny how many things about Rhonda seemed familiar to me. Like me, she loved dogs, lilacs, being out in the country; and she loved kids (she was a teacher). Like my mom, she had a strong faith. "I believe God leads us where we need to be," Rhonda told me. "We just have to trust Him. When my doctors told me I only had a 20 percent chance of survival even with a bone marrow transplant and no one in my family was a good match, I didn't give up. I kept praying. And God brought you to me."

I didn't know what to say. I hadn't looked at things quite that way before.

Randy and I thought about inviting Rhonda to our wedding, but since she didn't mention getting together I held off, hoping she'd be ready to meet someday.

The following spring Rhonda sent me an invitation to her June wedding to her high-school sweetheart, Kevin Jensen. In May I got a phone call from Rhonda's sister, Brenda. "I thought I'd surprise Rhonda and invite you to the shower I'm throwing her next Saturday," Brenda said. "If you'd like to come, I mean."

"Like to? I can't wait!"

That Saturday, Brenda had me hide in the bedroom. When Rhonda arrived, Brenda led me to the living room and announced, "Here's our other guest of honor."

Rhonda gasped. "Elly?" she whispered, her eyes suddenly glistening. Before I could answer, she threw her arms around me and gave me a long hug.

Stepping back, she said to the other guests, "This is Elly Bertrand—the woman who saved my life."

Everyone started clapping. "I'm just glad everything turned out okay," I said, embarrassed they were making a big deal out of something that had taken such little effort on my part. Rhonda was the one who'd really been brave.

It wasn't until a few weeks later, when I sat in a church practically blooming with lilacs and watched a radiant Rhonda walk down the aisle, that it hit me what a big deal the transplant really was. Rhonda now had a future to look forward to.

For the next year and a half Randy, the boys, and I moved several times, looking for a place that felt right. We wanted to stay in Mondovi for the boys' schools, and eventually we found a trailer home on a farm where I took over the care of the owner's herd of dairy cattle. Milking eighty-five cows twice a day got my blood pumping (now that my sons were hitting their teens, I needed the energy), and the rhythm of the work was oddly comforting.

Things for Rhonda weren't going so well. She tried to stay upbeat in her letters and phone calls, but I could hear a tiredness in her voice. It was Brenda who eventually told me that Rhonda was having health problems. The radiation treatment she'd needed before the transplant had damaged her kidneys.

Then one day I found out how desperate her situation really was. I went to check our mailbox, and inside was a thick envelope with Rhonda's handwriting. I opened it right away and started to read as I walked past the barns to our trailer.

"I have been praying for a way to go about telling you," Rhonda wrote in her five-page letter. She explained that her kidneys were failing, and her doctor had said her best chance for long-term survival was a kidney transplant. "A bone marrow donor is like a twin since they have the same immune system. My body would recognize your kidney as its own.... I feel bad presenting you with my situation when you have already done so much for me.... But I felt that I had to at least give you the option to decide if this would be something you'd be willing to consider."

I stopped dead in my tracks. *Donating bone marrow was simple,* I thought, *but how am I going to make this decision?* Rhonda had included the number of the transplant coordinator at the hospital where she'd gone for a consultation in case I needed it. I went inside and called.

"This transplant isn't something you should rush into," the coordinator warned me. "It means major surgery for you. Think about whether you want to go through the rest of your life with just one kidney. You could injure it in an accident, especially in your line of work."

I tucked Rhonda's letter in my jacket pocket and went to do the afternoon milking. As I tended to the cows, questions moved through my mind in almost the same rhythm, one after another. What would my boys do if something happened to me? What if one of them ever needed a kidney? What if I injured my remaining kidney? But what if I was Rhonda's only chance?

There was no way I could make this decision on my own. I knew where Mom and Rhonda would turn. *God, I'm not used to this,* I prayed, feeling a little unpracticed. *But I'm trusting this decision to You. Please let me know what to do.*

That night after the boys were in bed, I showed Randy the letter. "You know, my uncle donated a kidney to his brother thirty years ago, and both of them have been fine ever since," he said. "Whatever you decide, I'm behind you 100 percent."

Mom said she'd pray that I would come to the right decision, but the rest of my family bristled at the fact that Rhonda had even asked. "It's too risky," they insisted. "It's one thing to make a sacrifice like that for your own flesh and blood, but..."

The only time I could be alone to think was when I was doing the milking. For the next couple of weeks, every morning and afternoon, the long, narrow cowshed became my prayer chapel.

I read everything I could on kidney transplants—how an incision is made under the donor's ribs to remove the kidney, how it leaves a sizable scar, how the surgery is harder on the donor than the recipient and can require six weeks of recovery time. I'd been so frightened by a picture of a bone marrow aspiration needle, yet nothing I learned this time fazed me. That's when I knew. *God, I'm so at peace with this whole kidney-transplant thing, it must be what You want me to do.* I wasn't scared at all.

The fifth anniversary of our bone marrow transplant was coming up, the perfect time for me to let Rhonda know. I sent her a vase of silk lilacs, the same color as the real ones at her wedding, along with a note: "I think I've made my decision, but my family's against it. Pray for them to come around."

When she got the gift, Rhonda called, crying so hard she could barely speak.

Once I passed the pre-transplant medical tests and psychological evaluation, I told the boys. They were really proud of me, and by the time the transplant date arrived, the rest of my family was behind me too.

It felt good going into the operating room, knowing everyone I loved was supporting me. The surgery went well. Six hours later, a nurse had me up and walking. The next morning, I went down the hall to visit Rhonda.

She was sitting up in bed, a healthier glow on her face already. "Elly," she said, taking my hand, "I am so thankful God made someone as giving as you."

I knew how she felt. I was grateful to God too, for leading us, as Rhonda had told me, to where we needed to be. How else would an ordinary woman like me have ended up being a part of something so incredible?

Give Freely

If I can think of myself as loved, I can love and accept others. If I see myself as forgiven, I can be gracious toward others. If I see myself as powerful, I can do what I know is right. If I see myself as full, I can give myself freely to others.

KATHY PEEL

"Show Us What to Do"

BY ETHEL PERKINS

During the weeks when my husband was seriously ill, I tried desperately to keep our little picture-framing business running. One day our landlord told me that the building would be torn down. We had thirty days to vacate.

Thirty days! I was horrified. Del, my husband, was still in a wheelchair at the hospital, and I was running myself ragged trying to keep things together. "Lord, give me the strength to handle this," I would mumble while dashing back and forth.

I had a going-out-of-business sale, but as fast as the money came in, I'd take it with me to the hospital to pay the bills. Being self-employed, we had no medical insurance, no nest egg tucked away for catastrophic expenses. Finally the last day of the sale came at the same time Del was well enough to come home—still in a wheelchair, but learning how to walk with a cane.

We were both tremendously grateful for his recovery, and we should have been mighty happy. But unfortunately we weren't. We were broke. Our bank account was down to zero; we had no investments and no savings; and all the assets in the store were gone. Only the equity in our house remained.

A friend lent us $200, then a generous neighbor came over with his checkbook. We were grateful to those wonderful people, but how long does a few hundred dollars last when regular expenses keep coming? We were unable to borrow on the house, and we were both reluctant to borrow more from friends. How would we pay it back? Sell the house? But what then? We'd have no home plus no job and no business. We were both close to sixty, and we had nothing to live on. Our world looked very bleak.

That day, for the first time in our lives, we felt desperate. "What should we do?" I cried helplessly.

"God has helped us before," Del said suddenly. "He will do it again. Let's ask for guidance." He took my hand and I lowered myself to my knees beside him.

It must have been the touch of his hand—or faith from God coursing from his hand into mine—that sobered me. Del began. "Dear Lord, we are in an awful mess. We don't know which way to turn. Show us what to do." Together we prayed long and earnestly, and that night we slept peacefully, confident that the answer would come to us in some way soon.

The following morning I asked Del if he would like to take a drive to Santa Barbara, one hundred miles away. We had often gone there before, but Del had not taken a long drive since his illness. He said he would like to go, but that I should drive slowly so that he wouldn't become dizzy.

I packed a lunch, and we started out. Because I kept to the minimum speed allowed on freeways, I had to drive the car in the far right lane.

After we had driven about sixty-five miles, the freeway ran parallel to the ocean. We both commented on how beautiful the surf looked. Being so entranced with the view, I did not notice that the slow lane we were in became an "Exit Only" off-ramp leading to another freeway. By the time I realized my mistake, I couldn't swing back into the regular lane because several cars were passing us on our left.

"Oh, Del, we're on the wrong road," I said. "I'll turn around at the next exit." I felt annoyed at my blunder.

But there wasn't any off-ramp for quite a while. By the time we reached it, we saw inviting mountains ahead of us. "Why not go straight on?" Del suggested. "We don't have to go to Santa Barbara."

The freeway soon turned into an uphill, winding road, and every turn revealed a panorama of rolling hills hugged in by colorful mountains. "This is beautiful," I said. "Why haven't we ever come here before?" I continued driving, and soon we arrived at Ojai, a delightful little town steeped in Spanish history and architecture. I stopped the car on the main street and we just sat there, drinking in the quiet loveliness.

"Do you feel what I feel?" Del asked softly. "This is where we belong." I didn't answer; it wasn't necessary. Each of us knew how the other felt.

We went to a real-estate office along the main street and told our story. "We need a home where we can run a very small business," Del explained.

The broker's answer was as incredible as that wrong turn in the road turned out to be. "There's a framing shop here," he said, "and the owners are moving East in a few weeks. Just across the street there's a little house for sale, with a workshop in the rear. It's on a lovely, shaded street, but since it's C-1 property, you can have both a residence and business there."

We drove over to see it and immediately fell in love with it. Everything was perfect—the price, the location, the facilities. We explained that we had to sell our house first. At that time, we didn't even have ten dollars to put down on it.

Driving home again, we prayed all the way, again asking for guidance. "If we're supposed to move to Ojai, God, tell us what to do to make this possible." The answer came to us loud and clear. In fact, we were so confident that when we erected that FOR SALE sign on the front lawn, the house was—in our minds—already sold. The house sold in three days.

That was almost eight years ago, and we have been happier here in Ojai than at any other time in our lives. Our semi-retirement is sheer joy, with plenty of time to take trips and vacations.

Sometimes we ask ourselves, "Why didn't we come here sooner?" But we know the answer. We had to experience hardship and desperation before we were humble enough to get down on our knees. We had to ask God what we should do, instead of telling Him what we wanted Him to do for us. Once we had done that, God was able to perform His wonders. For us, my wrong turn on the road was God's right turn for our lives.

Lead Me, Lord

Show me your ways, O Lord, teach me your paths.
Guide me in your truth and teach me, for you are
God my Savior, and my hope is in you all day long.

PSALM 25:4–5 NIV

Meet the Winans

BY CeCe Winans

S inging and praising come as natural as breathing in my family. Long before my brothers hit the stage as the Winans, we were praising up a storm together. Mom and Dad loved letting loose with a good gospel song, and they passed that on to all ten of us kids. We sang at home, we sang in the choir at the Mount Zion Church of God in Christ, and we sang in the car on the way there and back.

It was the 1960s. We grew up with the Motown sound in the Motor City. You know, The Temptations, Smokey Robinson, The Supremes. That sweet soul music! But only at other folks' houses. To Mom and Dad music meant church music, plain and simple. Singing is a holy thing for everyone in our family.

It's like my brother Ronald, who's the second oldest, taught me. I was eight years old and very shy. Our church choir was getting ready to perform "I've Been Rejoicing Every Day." Ronald told me I had to do the solo.

"You can do it, CeCe," he said. "You've been given a gift. Use it to praise the Lord. You've got to lead this song."

Singing solo in front of my family was one thing, but a church full of people? No way.

Ronald kept working on me, encouraging me to use my gift, and reminding me that my singing was really about letting God work through me. "You've got to do this for the Lord," he said.

Finally I gave in. Time came for our performance. I was so nervous! The words to the solo flew right out of my head. But I kept Ronald's advice in my mind. I managed to open my mouth and let my love for the Lord flow out. The solo took care of itself.

I'm not so shy anymore. These days I do a lot of singing on my own—without my family. But every time I'm about to step onstage, I remember what Ronald told me. Then I get out there and get lost in my love for the Lord.

The biggest lesson my brother taught me about faith was just a few years back. Ronald started getting short of breath. Bronchitis, the doctor thought. It didn't clear up, though.

Finally, our brother Marvin got Ronald to visit a specialist in Ann Arbor, Michigan. "You've had a heart attack," the doctor told him. "Your aorta is on the verge of rupturing. I can't believe you were even able to walk in here."

They admitted Ronald to the University of Michigan Medical Center and scheduled him for surgery first thing the next morning. Our whole family—Mom, Dad, all us siblings, plus plenty of nieces and nephews—hotfooted it up to Ann Arbor. The hospital was packed with Winans.

Ronald was heavily sedated to keep him as still as possible. He was on oxygen, IVs, and all kinds of monitors. The doctor pulled the immediate family members aside. "Ronald is going to die whether we operate or not," he told us. "I think we should wake him up now so you all can say your good-byes."

"Doctor," Dad said, "you just do your best. Meanwhile, we're going to do what we do best."

Mom, Dad, and the rest of the family crowded into the hospital chapel. We prayed and sang one gospel song after another. We lifted the roof off that little church! All night long it went like that. We even took shifts so the prayers would not stop for a moment.

The next morning the doctor said, "Something strange happened over the night. Ronald's vitals are much better today. I'd say he now has a 50 percent chance of pulling through the operation. Don't ask me to explain it."

He didn't have to explain. We knew.

Several hours into the operation the doctor came to talk to us again. "We're doing everything we can," he said. "But it doesn't look good. Ronald's heart is terribly damaged. It basically exploded on the operating table. You need to be prepared for the worst."

The doctor turned to leave. My dad asked, "Doc, is it all right if we pray for you?"

The surgeon looked surprised. He nodded. "Sure," he said.

We gathered around the doctor and put our hands on him. "Lord," my father said, "we know that You can do anything. Let this gifted man see our Ronald through to another day of precious life."

The doctor rushed back into the OR, and all of us marched down to the chapel. We repented amongst ourselves so that there was nothing in our hearts or spirits to hold us back. We let the

Lord work through us, crying and singing out to the Lord, using our voices to draw Hs mighty power closer.

Something happened in that hospital. I'd spent my whole life singing the Lord's praises, but never before had I felt so strongly what Ronald had taught me as a child. God really was using us, each and every one, to do His work.

And do His work He did! Ronald made it through the operation. The hospital staff was amazed. Over the next hours the doctor gave us updates on Ronald's chances of survival. The percentage just kept rising. Meanwhile, the singing and the praying never let up.

Two days after the operation Ronald opened his eyes. They let us all into his room. You could feel the love in the air. The whole hospital was thick with the perfume of the Holy Spirit.

Today I'm glad to say that Ronald is back to his old self, praising God with the rest of us. Singing and praising. I guess you could say that to us Winans, they're as natural as breathing—and as vital.

A Song of Joy

Through all eternity to Thee
A joyful song I'll raise;
For oh! eternity's too short
To utter all Thy praise.

JOSEPH ADDISON

Spring Break?

BY DAWN MEEHAN

I t was the third day of spring break—a break for my kids, not me. I am a stay-at-home mom of six kids (seven, if you count my husband, Joe), and they wanted to let me know what a good time they were having—as early in the morning and as loudly as possible. Who needs an alarm clock when you have fourteen-year-old Austin and ten-year-old Jackson tearing through the house, yelling at the top of their lungs (the only volume at which a kid can yell inside the house) and whipping pillows at each other first thing in the a.m.? Good morning!

Our television had been broken for three weeks. The part we needed to fix it was apparently being delivered by water buffalo. Joe's car was in the shop. "You don't mind if I take the van, do you?" he'd said the night before. No, of course not. Being cooped up in the house with six kids and no TV to occupy them has always been my idea of fun.

I got out of bed, dreading what the day might bring. At least the weather was warm—46 degrees, which almost qualified as tropical in Chicago in April. I'd been praying for the snow to melt, so I could send the kids outside to play and burn off some energy.

I walked into the kitchen, spilled cereal crunching underfoot, and made myself a cup of coffee.

"Can we go outside and play?" my three youngest asked.

"Sure," I said, opening the kitchen door and releasing them. Well, even if the sky said Antarctica, the calendar said it was spring. Another cup of coffee and I might be brave enough to help Savannah, twelve, my oldest daughter, tackle the mess in her bedroom.

Savannah likes her room nice and neat. She shares a room with Lexi, seven, who prefers disarray.

"Don't worry, Savannah," I said. "I'll help you shovel a path to your bed." We unearthed Barbie dolls, Barbie dresses, Barbie's car and washing machine, a headless Barbie (Clayton's handiwork?), Community Chest cards from Monopoly (oh, that's where those went), wrapping paper from a birthday party two months before, and a hard brown object that looked suspiciously like a petrified hot dog. It was an archaeological dig with the oldest stuff at the bottom. Savannah burrowed under a crumpled Snow White costume and emerged triumphant. "My hairbrush!"

Then Jackson walked into the room carrying a snow shovel. "Look what I found," he said. Lying motionless at the end of the shovel was an opossum. It looked dead or maybe it was just playing possum...how could you tell the difference? I wasn't about to find out.

"Jackson," I said in a calm and collected voice, "WHAT ARE YOU DOING?! Why would you scoop up a wild animal and bring it into the house? Use your brain, boy!"

Jackson turned and the shovel tipped precariously. Great, the possibly deceased opossum was going to fall on the floor.

"Take that back outside this minute," I ordered. "And leave it outside." Just in case he got any different ideas. (What is it with boys and critters, anyway?)

I finished up in the girls' room and headed back to the kitchen with a big bag of garbage. I stopped in my tracks. The floor was covered in muddy footprints. I'd prayed for the snow to melt. Here was my answer.

Where were the paper towels? I looked at the counter. Breadcrumbs, open jars of peanut butter and jelly, bowls, spoons, whisks, and measuring cups covered the counter where Savannah had mixed up a pan of extra-gooey brownies. I think it's great that my kids can cook. Someday they will learn to clean up too.

All I could find were the diaper wipes. I used those to scrub the mud off the floor, when Brooklyn, my three-year-old, wandered in from the yard.

"Where's your coat?" I asked her.

"Outside," she answered. "I don't need it. It's hot."

"And your shoes?"

"Outside."

"It's 46 degrees. Practically swimming weather."

"I go swimming!" Brooklyn said excitedly. Not until she got her diaper changed. And I had the wipe right in my hand. I went out to throw the dirty diaper away—only to discover the kids had taken their food outside for a picnic. In the mud.

ZZZZZZZZZZ. The dryer made the pleasant noise it does when a load is finished. I dashed in to take the clothes out. Shirts, pants, socks, and sweats. (Somewhere between baby number three and baby number four I stopped sorting laundry.) Dabs of brilliant purple covered everything. I scratched at it, and it stuck to my hand. Ah, gum. Gum on socks and pants and sweatshirts.

"Who left gum in their pocket?" I shouted, even though I knew who the culprits were: I Dunno and Not Me.

Brooklyn came trotting out in her bathing suit. Let's see.

Muddy footprints crisscrossing the kitchen floor. Check.

Gum stuck to a dozen articles of just-laundered clothing. Check.

Dishes piled up to the ceiling. Check.

Baby wearing a bathing suit in 46-degree weather. Check.

Opossum on a shovel. Check.

A typical day at our house, never mind the added bedlam of spring break.

Lexi darted past me wailing, "Mom, Jackson hit me."

Jackson, hot on her trail, retorted, "Yeah, well, she shot a Nerf dart at my ear."

"It was an accident." "Was not!" "Was too!" "Was not!" "Was too!"

I looked at the clock. Only four days, eighteen hours and twenty-three minutes until they went back to school. More importantly, only one more hour until my husband would get home from work, at which point I would tender my resignation and board a plane for Bora Bora. I don't know where Bora Bora is, but I bet they don't have opossums there.

An hour later Joe got home and asked, "So what did you do all day?"

That's when I locked myself in our bedroom to pray for serenity, I mean, fold some laundry. I didn't want to be a mother anymore. What was I doing this for? I was tired of settling arguments, cleaning floors, chasing down orphan socks, and coaxing a three-year-old out of her bathing suit into warmer clothes. God would have to find some other profession for me. Lion tamer would be fine. In fact, lion tamer wasn't so far from what I was doing already.

I heard a small scratching sound in the hallway. I looked over at the door and saw a folded piece of paper being slipped under it. What now? I went over and picked the paper up. I unfolded it. There was a crayon drawing of the eight of us, holding hands and smiling. "I love you, Mommy," was written on the bottom. "You're the best Mommy in the world. Love, Lexi."

A smile tugged at the corners of my mouth, and the stress of the day began to melt away. I gazed at the drawing and thought about the kids' impromptu picnic in the mud. Okay, even I'd said 46 degrees was balmy for April in Chicago. I recalled the brownies Savannah had made. *I've taught my kids to cook and they like it—I must be doing something right.* Then I pictured the opossum on the shovel and that just cracked me up. What did I need TV for? I was part of the most amazing reality show on earth!

All at once I heard giggling coming from the other side of the door. Little fingers poked under it. I was about to go over and tickle those little fingers. But there was something I needed to do first. I thanked God for giving me these moments to remind me why I do this. For the joy. For the love. For each and every one of my six children.

Now if He could only get them to stop bringing me opossums on a shovel.

It's Worth It!

Children are like sponges:
They absorb all your strength and leave you limp.
But give 'em a squeeze and you get it all back.

Golden Apples

BY MARIAN VOGEL

My father pulled into the parking lot next to the sprawling gray asylum. Windows barred, it was as cold and grim as the phone call I had received four days earlier: "Mrs. Vogel, this is the Connecticut State Police. Your husband has had a mental breakdown. He abandoned his truck on Route 95."

My husband, Ron, was a long-distance trucker with Yellow Freight. When I called to tell the company about Ron's breakdown, his bosses assured me he wouldn't lose his job and that they would pay for help for him. Dad and Mom brought me from Pennsylvania to pick up Ron and take him to a small private hospital closer to home.

I got out of the car and slumped against the door. My mind was swirling with the words, *It's your fault; you're to blame.* My mouth was dry as cotton. Even if I went in I couldn't comfort Ron.

Dad touched my elbow. "Come, Marian. It will be all right. We'll help you." But it wasn't all right. My marriage had gone sour, and I knew that one cause of Ron's breakdown was the strain of our constant bickering.

We trudged around the building, finally finding an entrance that opened into a dingy sitting room. After a few minutes Ron slouched in warily, heavily medicated, his shoulders hunched as if he were trying to retreat inside himself. His clothes were wrinkled. He needed a bath.

He took my arm and held on. "How are you? How are the children?" he asked over and over with a forlorn look in his eyes.

Before we left, a doctor took us aside and told us that Ron had had a psychotic break, as well as paranoid delusions. Convinced of impending disaster, he had driven for miles blowing his truck's air horn and blinking his lights, thinking he was warning people. As he sped along, he threw everything out of his truck, including money. Finally he abandoned the truck and was taken to the police station and then transported by ambulance to the asylum.

As Dad and I drove Ron to the private hospital, I glanced from my husband's haunted eyes to the calm, self-assured profile of my father. I wished, not for the first time, that Ron was more like him. I longed for warmth and affection, even flowers once in a while like my father brought to my mother. But Ron was a proud, private man, and our petty arguments and caustic exchanges had made him even more distant.

Over the weeks that followed, Ron was in and out of the hospital. Finally, stabilized on lithium, he was able to go back to driving for Yellow Freight. I asked his doctor how long it would take for Ron to get over his depression. The doctor said, "Even on medication, Ron is likely to have a psychotic break about every two years." My future yawned before me like a black hole—a loveless marriage to a mentally unstable man incapable of affection.

To make it easier for Ron we moved our three young children from a farm in the Pocono Mountains to a small house closer to the Yellow Freight offices in East Petersburg. But we were country folk, and we missed the farm terribly. Ron had enjoyed farm chores but shrank from his suburban role, leaving me to do all the work. He'd plunk down in front of the television on Saturday mornings and I'd say, "Ron, you're king of the couch potatoes. Can't you mow the lawn just once? My mother never had to tell Daddy to mow the lawn!"

"Well, you never have any trouble telling me, do you?" Ron would answer acidly. "Why don't you practice what you preach in those songs you're always singing about love, peace, and joy? Why don't you bring us a little joy, Marian?"

Then I'd mow the lawn.

For the year following Ron's breakdown, this was our life. He was too depressed to do anything but drive his truck. I plodded through life caring for the children and trying to do all the chores around the house. Time after time I berated Ron, then was tormented by thoughts that I might be driving him to another breakdown. My own depression and anxiety seemed unbearable.

The day came when I felt I couldn't go on any longer. After Ron left for work, I turned to wash the dishes; I would leave the house spotless. The car waited in the closed garage with a full tank of gas. I'd turn on the engine and be overcome by fumes long before anyone found me.

The telephone rang. I snatched it, on the first ring, wondering why I had answered it.

"How are you, Marian?" It was my brother, Joel. I hadn't talked to him in a few weeks.

"I'm fine, Joel. Just fine."

"Marian, are you thinking of taking your life?"

I gasped. "What? Who told you that?" How could he have known?

"Just now I had a strong feeling that you were in danger. I believe it was a message from God. Marian, we need to pray about this right now."

I listened transfixed as Joel earnestly begged God to help me. Then we talked until Joel was satisfied I was out of immediate danger. He suggested I go with the children to Mom and Dad's for a while to do some healing away from Ron.

I hung up and leaned against the same counter where I had contemplated my death. The frying pan was soaking in the sink. My hands shaking, I scoured it clean and pulled the plug. As the dirty suds swirled down the drain, so did my desire for death. I marveled that Joel had called at the moment I needed him most. Only God could have inspired that call. I felt a strange peace. *Marian*, I told myself, *you may have nothing else, but you have God. He will be your strength.*

I telephoned my parents, who lived several hours away, and they agreed that I should stay with them for a while. The children enrolled in school near my parents' house.

Three miserable months passed. My parents were kind and loving; but I felt like a failure as a wife, mother, and human being. I worried about Ron's mental state as he lived alone, but knew we'd settle into the same old pattern if I returned.

One June evening I knelt by my bed as the white curtains billowed in a soft breeze. "Lord, please change Ron. Give him a new heart. Please, God, so I can go back to him." I began to cry.

I heard my name. *"Marian."* The voice seemed to fill the entire room, yet I immediately sensed that no one else could hear it. The voice went on. *"Before I change Ron, you must change. From now on I don't want you to think one bad thought about Ron. I want you to praise him, compliment him, and build him up. I will help you."*

I crawled into bed and curled up. Breathing in deeply, I fell sound asleep. As the morning sun flooded my room, I awoke feeling cleansed and renewed. The children and I returned to Ron.

When Ron came through the door from the garage that first evening, I was in the kitchen. I hadn't let him know that we were coming. He stood with his hand on the doorknob, his expression unsure. I went over and kissed him. He hugged me and said, "I'm glad you're home, Marian."

Things were different now. They had to be. My grandpa Hershey always used to say, "A word fitly spoken is like apples of gold in a setting of silver" (Proverbs 25:11 NRSV). I decided to give Ron "apples of gold." He was a hard worker and a good provider. I started telling him so and thanking him.

It was an uphill battle. There were days I felt my old negativity and anger surging back, and I wanted to run away. Instead I ran to God. If I needed to complain, I didn't lash out at Ron; I took my frustrations to God.

I became increasingly aware of Ron's sensitivity and the depth of his feelings, his unconditional love for the children, and his neatness around the house and in the way he dressed. I thanked him for it all.

Gradually Ron began smiling, then teasing, but in a playful way. I complimented him on his sense of humor. I cooked his favorites—cornmeal mush for breakfast and pork, sauerkraut, and dumplings for dinner.

One night Ron lingered at the table over a second piece of shoofly pie. He talked about how learning difficulties had made his childhood unhappy—how hard it had been to take the constant criticism. Suddenly he put his hand over mine and, haltingly, began to pray. "Lord, I thank You for all our blessings. Most especially I thank You for Marian and for the love You've given back to us."

We began praying together for Ron to be rid of his depression. Gradually his doctor reduced the dosage of his medications. Then he took him off lithium altogether and instead prescribed a mild pill on an as-needed basis. Returning home from one doctor's appointment, Ron said, "I think God has healed me." I searched his face. His eyes were calm and assured.

One night Ron shuffled into the kitchen with a grin as wide as his Yellow Freight truck. He was carrying a big bouquet of flowers. He held them out to me. I ran to hug him, my tears splashing onto the red carnations and baby's breath. "Watch it," he said, laughing, "or these flowers will start to grow."

Sixteen years have passed since Ron's breakdown. He's never had another. Eventually our marriage became a real joy, although it didn't happen overnight. But I knew it would from the moment that June night when God called my name and then taught me how to give golden apples.

Put On Love

Therefore, as God's chosen people, holy and dearly loved, clothe yourselves with compassion, kindness, humility, gentleness and patience.... Forgive as the Lord forgave you. And over all these virtues put on love, which binds them all together in perfect unity.

COLOSSIANS 3:12–14 NIV

Handbags!

BY MARY NORTON

Micah and Reilly—my daughters, ages three and one—wouldn't stop crying. Or tossing their Froot Loops onto the floor. Or making messes. Or waking me at all hours of the night until I felt like a zombie. I'd dreamed of motherhood all my life, prayed for healthy, beautiful children with my husband, Joe. Yet now that I had Moo and Roo—that's what we nicknamed them—I could barely function.

Postpartum depression, my doctor called it. "You'd be surprised how many new mothers suffer from it," he said. "For years we didn't have a name for it."

I had all the classic symptoms: I was stressed out, irritable, and liable to burst into tears at any moment. Low self-esteem? Try nonexistent. Pre-motherhood I'd been a successful movie-production coordinator. And now? I was a failed mother. I could barely take care of my babies—much less myself. I felt like I was going through life with my eyes barely open and all the color faded from the world.

"I miss my work. I miss being good at something," I told my doctor. "I feel so guilty!"

"You'll find a way to work and be a great mother too," he assured me. "Just be patient." Meanwhile, he wrote me a prescription and told me to go easy on myself.

I cried all the way home. Work? When would I find the time? I barely had time for Joe, who worked long hours at a restaurant. My mom would have told me to pray. But I had what I'd prayed for—two beautiful, healthy children. Now I wanted to ask God to help me do something that should have come naturally? It didn't seem right. Still, sitting in traffic at a long light, I stared at the center of my steering wheel and prayed. *Lord, lead me to my dreams.*

That night, as always, I fell asleep exhausted. I'd never been one to dream a lot, much less remember my dreams. But as I slept I saw the most wonderful story unfold. It was like a fairy tale made real.

I walked through a field of brilliantly colored flowers. Yellow daffodils. Pink daisies. Green orchids. Such vibrant hues. I bent down, gathered an armful of flowers, and inhaled their aroma. I felt like Dorothy, exploring the land of Oz. All at once I sat on the ground and started weaving the stems together. I'm not the knitting type. I'd never so much as sewn a pot holder. But somehow, I fashioned the flowers into bouquet-like handbags.

"My," I said to myself. They were impossibly beautiful. Looking at the handbags, I felt contentment flow over me. How could handbags make me so happy?

Suddenly it was morning. I was sure the feeling would vanish. But it didn't. I held on to it as I fixed Joe's breakfast. It was still there after he kissed me good-bye.

As I cleaned up the kitchen I thought, *I want to make one of those handbags or at least something that reminds me of them.* A pretty strange thought, since I'm not big on handbags. I had just one evening bag and it was plain, functional brown. Still, I couldn't shake the idea. *Okay,* I finally decided, *I'll decorate some handbags. If they turn out awful, I'll just toss them out.*

I dug up forty dollars, strapped Moo and Roo into their car seats, and headed for the department store. In the accessories aisle I found a shelf of handbags.

Next, a fabric shop. A bolt of lime-green material seemed to jump out at me. I took it to the cutting table, where a roll of pink ribbon lay. I held the fabric to the ribbon. The colors danced. I added the ribbon to my cart. And then handfuls of decorative glass beads. "Aren't these pretty, girls?" I asked Moo and Roo. The kids giggled agreeably and smiled and drooled.

My last stop was a fancy silk flower shop. I was running out of cash. "Do you have any samples lying around?" I asked the clerk. She rummaged around and held up a stem of green silk orchids. "How about this? We'll never use it."

Oh, but I will! I thought. Standing in the checkout line I wondered, *How do I know that?* With the production company I was always on the business side. I never did anything "creative."

Just numbers and schedules. This was an completely new feeling; one I had to follow.

Back home, I dumped my supplies onto the dining room table. It looked like a giant jigsaw puzzle. Now what? I closed my eyes and thought of my dream. I snipped some of the lime fabric and glued it to a handbag. I added some pink ribbon and a few of the green orchids. I cleared off the table and set the purse upright. I backed up a few steps and looked critically at what I'd done. *Am I nuts or is this not half bad?*

The girls went down for their nap and instead of napping too, I went back to the table. I matched fabric with ribbon and flowers. By late afternoon, I'd finished three handbags. Goofy, maybe, but I felt like a million bucks. *Thank You, God, for helping me feel better.*

The handbags were still on the table the next day when my babysitter, Lauren, stopped by. She managed a local boutique. "Did you make these?" she asked.

"Yes. Can you believe it?"

"They're darling! Let me take them to the shop. You never know. Someone might buy them." I thought she was kidding. But she insisted, so I gave them to her. Two days later the phone rang. It was Lauren. "Got any more bags?" she asked.

I packed up the girls and returned to the stores. The materials seemed to leap into my hands, as if right from my dream. Bolts of fabric. Glass beads. Handfuls of silk orchids. All with the approval of Moo and Roo. Back home, I went to work again.

"You need a name for your handbags," Lauren said. "Something as bright and original and fun as the bags are." Lauren looked down at the girls sitting on the floor—one banging her rattle on a spoon, the other hugging her bear. "Something like Moo Roo."

Moo Roo handbags it was. I was in business. But not anything I could have ever dreamed—or something I could only have dreamed. Soon I had an order from a department store with thirteen locations.

The best was yet to come. A few days before the Emmys, a friend from the film industry dropped by. He took some of my bags. "I want to show them to Julia Louis-Dreyfus's stylist," he said.

I laughed. "Sure, go ahead."

A week later I was in the checkout line at the grocery store. I grabbed a magazine to pass the time. I couldn't believe it. There was a huge picture of Julia Louis-Dreyfus—and she was carrying one of my green orchid bags! The next thing I knew, I was showing my bags at a New York trade show. I came back with $65,000 in orders. Amazingly, Moo Roo handbags were a hit.

As I said, I don't dream much and I never had that particular dream again. It was as if a vision had been put before me and my eyes opened. Then again, maybe those are the best dreams of all—the ones we don't see coming, even if Someone else did.

The Best Dreams

Delight yourself in the LORD,
and he will give you the desires of your heart.
Commit your way to the LORD;
trust in him, and he will act.

PSALM 37:4-5 ESV

Love to Spare

BY DELILAH

Settling into my chair in the broadcast booth, I slip on my headphones and adjust the big yellow mike, then give my producer a thumbs-up through the window. I glance at the clock: 7:00 p.m. Time for my radio show, *Delilah After Dark*. Buttons on the console start blinking, calls coming in from listeners across the country. I push a button and say, "Hello, this is Delilah. How are you doing tonight?"

"My wife's away on a business trip, and I really miss her. I was wondering, could you play something to let her know I'm thinking about her?"

What a sweet, romantic gesture... "Sure," I tell the caller, signaling my producer and sound engineer to cue up "Wind Beneath My Wings."

I say hi to another listener. "Delilah, I really need someone to talk to. My marriage is falling apart, and I'm worried what it's doing to my kids." When she tells me about the hurt and anger that have swept over her house, I ask her, "Have you thought about getting counseling for your kids? And yourself. You don't have to go through this alone."

"Maybe...," she says slowly.

"I'm going to play a song for you. Call me back in a couple weeks and let me know how you're doing, okay?"

"I will. Thanks for listening."

Hoping I've helped that caller, I sit back as "You've Got a Friend" goes out over the airwaves. When we break for the local news, I take off my headphones and pick up the phone to check on my own kids. "Hi, Doug," I say to my husband. "Did TJ get back home from basketball practice? Is Zacky asleep yet?" I ask after Sonny, Manny, Tangi, and Shaylah too. It's always an adventure having six kids in the house!

"TJ wants you to know he hit a three-pointer. Zacky dozed off halfway through his mashed bananas. Shaylah found her inhaler." Doug laughs. "Everyone's doing fine, Dee, don't worry."

We hang up, and I say a prayer for the woman who'd called me earlier to tell me about her marriage troubles. As blessed as my life is now, I understand where people like her are coming from. I've been there myself.

Growing up in small-town Oregon with an alcoholic dad and a codependent mom, I knew all about living in a house ripe with hurt and anger. My refuge was the local radio station, where I'd apprenticed since the owners heard me in a speech contest and decided a girl who liked to talk that much had to be on air.

Radio was how I survived when I ran off to Seattle after my dad kicked me out for breaking curfew. I married young—too young to know the difference between wanting the big happy family I never had growing up and being truly ready for the kind of commitment that would take. The one good thing that came of the marriage was my baby, Sonny, whom I loved with a completeness I'd never imagined possible. I threw myself into being the best mom and best DJ I could be. I landed my own show and really got involved talking to the people who called in to me with song requests and finding out more about their lives.

I should have been paying a lot closer attention to my own life, should have seen that the eating binges and diet pills provided only paltry relief at best from the pain of my failing marriage.

My brother, Matt, tried to get through to me. "Take your problems to God," Matt urged. "He'll always be there." Yeah, right. So where was he when Matt and his wife were killed in a plane crash? When my husband walked out on me? When the station manager fired me for playing songs that were too sentimental?

In a matter of months, I'd lost almost everything that I cared about. I felt a deep pain that food and pills and the string of men I dated couldn't touch. Only when Sonny looked up at me, his dark eyes full of trust, did I find some solace. *But I'm such a mess*, I thought. *Do I even deserve his love?*

Late one night while remembering my brother's words, I broke down. "I can't go on like this," I said. "God, if You're real and You care about me, I need to know."

The next day I went to Pike Place Market to do some grocery shopping. Going back to my car, I noticed something stuck beneath the windshield wiper. I looked around at the other cars in the lot. Nothing on their windshields. *It figures*, I thought. *I'm the only one who gets a ticket.* I got nearer and saw that tucked under my wiper was a tiny book—a Bible. I took it off the car and opened it. Inside someone had written the words "Jesus Loves You." I stood there, my hand shaking so hard the pages of the Bible rattled. Could this be the God my brother had been trying to tell me about? Someone who was always with us, who loved us, whether we knew it or not?

I started going to the church just at the end of my street. A friend there took me to my first 12 Step meeting. That night I stood up in a room full of people I didn't know and for the first time talked openly about my unhealthy relationships with my parents, men, pills, and food. The more of these meetings I went to, the more I felt the incredible sense of connection that comes when people share their lives with one another. Fellowship, some people called it. To me, it was God using us to spread His love.

I braved a move all the way across the country to host a nighttime radio show in Boston. One of the first things I did was find a church. That's where I met Doug, the man I would marry. Not that I realized it then. Sure, he was cute, and good with Sonny. But given my romantic history, I'd decided to focus on my son and my career. Doug and I were casual friends for a while before we had our first real conversation. I noticed then how much Doug made me laugh, plus he talked about how as an only child, he'd always wanted a house full of kids. *This is the kind of person I want to build a future with,* I thought.

Doug and I had been married just over a year when our daughter Shaylah was born. I had secretly feared I couldn't love a child as completely as I had my first. But the minute I held my golden-haired baby girl to my breast, I started to fall in love. *Thank You, God,* I prayed. *It's good to know there's always room in my heart for another child.*

We moved back to Seattle so I could do *Delilah After Dark.* Once we settled in, Doug and I found ourselves talking about turning our family of four into more. "There are so many kids who need homes," I said, "who need love." I wanted to adopt a child other people might not consider, and Doug agreed. We wanted to be sure, though, that bringing a new child into our home would not hurt Sonny and Shaylah in any way.

One day Sonny said wistfully, "It would be nice to have a brother my own age." It was all the nudging we needed.

Doug and I signed up with an adoption agency and had to go through extensive screening before our caseworker would tell us about a child. "He's twelve, badly abused by his parents." She handed us a photo of a boy with a shy yet beguiling grin. "His name is Emmanuel. Manny for short. Why don't you take the weekend to think about it?"

We took the photo home and put it on our refrigerator. "I want to see," three-year-old Shaylah said. I lifted her up. "Shay, that's Emmanuel. He needs a home. Daddy and I are praying about whether it's right to have him live with us."

That Sunday in church the choir started singing, "God be with us, so close to us, Emmanuel...." Shaylah tugged at my sleeve. "Mommy," she whispered, "they're singing about my new brother!"

First thing Monday morning we called up the adoption agency. "We're sure. When can we meet Manny?"

We took Sonny with us on our first visit to Manny's foster home. We all talked for a while, then the boys went down to the rec room to play video games. Pretty soon we heard them busting out laughing. Manny started coming over for weekends, then longer. By the time we were given custody of Manny, it was hard to imagine our lives without him piggybacking Shaylah around or battling it out with Sonny on the chessboard.

I was watching one of their games when Manny said, "I wish TJ and Tangi could be with us too." TJ and Tangi were his brother and sister, ages nine and eleven.

Even though Doug and I were expecting our second baby, we went to see our caseworker. "I know you mean well," she said, "but you don't understand the kind of deep-seated problems TJ and Tangi have. They've been through a whole string of foster homes. Tangi has temper tantrums. TJ's been kicked out of school so many times I've lost count." She paused and gave me a long look, her eyes dropping to my rounded belly. "You're pregnant and you want to take on more children? I don't think you have any more room in your lives."

"Yes, we do!" I cried. "Just give us a chance with Tangi and TJ."

We started out with short visits, which went better than we'd hoped, especially with TJ, who seemed hungry to be part of a family again. It nearly broke my heart when he asked, "Can I call you Mom since I don't have a real mom anymore?"

Then a crisis at their foster home sent TJ and Tangi to stay with us sooner than anyone had anticipated. "The kids are really confused about what's going to happen to them now," the caseworker warned us when she dropped them off. "They're going to act out." It didn't take long. I asked TJ to clean his room. He exploded, tearing up everything that he could lay his hands on.

For a moment, I stood in the doorway, paralyzed, remembering my father's alcoholic rages and how I'd been powerless to stop them. Then I remembered something I'd heard in a parenting class about how kids in TJ's situation would lash out to test our love.

God, help me show TJ that we won't stop loving him any more than You'll stop loving us.

"TJ," I said, "maybe it's hard for you to believe right now, but Dad and I aren't going to go away. We love you, and we want to be your forever family." TJ didn't respond. I could only pray that he had heard what I had said to him.

Seven months into my pregnancy, the doctor put me on complete bed rest. One morning I woke to the smell of frying sausage. A few minutes later, TJ walked into my bedroom carrying a tray. "Morning, Mom," he said softly. I half sat up.

On the tray were two fried eggs, yolks runny the way I like them, sausage, and toast.

"Did Dad cook breakfast?" I asked.

"No, I did. I wanted to surprise you."

It took a little longer for Tangi. She was gentle and calm with baby Zacky, born two months after she moved in. Otherwise, there were tantrums on a daily basis. Doug and I had no idea how to cope with her moods. Sometimes Tangi wouldn't even talk to us.

The caseworker called us in. She said, "We know that you have done your best, but we don't think you're capable of meeting TJ's and Tangi's needs. We're going to place them with experienced foster parents who are specially trained to deal with dysfunctional children."

God, I thought You said that love never fails. Why aren't we getting through to Tangi then? I asked. *Why are they taking her and TJ away?*

That same night I invited Tangi to come over to the radio station with me to help me watch Zacky. She was thrilled to be trusted with the baby, but once he dozed off on the way home, Tangi withdrew again. A painful silence filled the car. I heard a sniffle.

I glanced at Tangi. Even in the darkness, I could see tears glistening on her face. Suddenly she let out a cry that was raw with pain. I pulled the car over to the side of the road, and she collapsed into my arms, sobbing.

Out poured the story of how frightened she'd been living with her biological mother, whose boyfriend had hurt her and her brothers. "But this hurts even worse. You and Dad are my family. They can't make me leave!"

Next morning Doug and I called up the caseworker. "TJ and Tangi belong here with us," we said. "How can we make them a part of our family forever? We'll do whatever it takes."

That's how it came to be that now, when I sit back during a break and call home to check on the kids, I have six to ask after: Sonny, Shaylah, Manny, Tangi, TJ, and Zacky. My forever family.

The buttons on the console are blinking again. I slip my headphones back on, ready to say hello to more listeners. I can't wait to talk to them about their lives—and to share part of mine. Especially some of the love I have been so uncommonly blessed with.

Love that Unites

Lord, behold our family here assembled.
We thank You for this place in which we dwell,
for the love that unites us...
for the health, the work, the food, and the bright skies
that make our lives delightful;
for our friends in all parts of the earth. Amen.

ROBERT LOUIS STEVENSON

A New Trust

BY CATHY BRAMMER

The other nurses at the hospital were happy. And why not? It was Valentine's Day. Everyone had plans. I tried to ignore the flowers, candy, and balloons, and concentrate on the stack of home health referrals on my desk. *Lord, all I did was give, give, give. I was with that man for twenty-nine years. And after all that time he just up and left me for another woman.*

I finished up about 7:00 p.m. and headed for the parking lot. I spotted a few other hospital workers hurrying for their cars. One nurse I recognized held a box of flowers under her arm while she fumbled around in her bag for her keys. *Probably has a candlelit dinner waiting for her.* The only thing waiting for me was an empty house and a frozen dinner to throw into the microwave.

I pulled into my driveway about twenty minutes later and sat staring at the house while the moon slid behind some clouds. *This was supposed to be our dream home,* I thought. A part of me dreaded going inside, to a place where it seemed my dreams had deserted me. Finally, I forced myself out of the car, up the walk, and through the door. I pulled off my coat.

There was the bookcase Gene and I had picked out together. Now it was filled with all my self-help books. *Lot of good those did.* I peeked into our son's room. Tony didn't live here anymore, but it had always been nice for me to know there was a place for him when he'd come to visit. In our bedroom—it was still hard to think of it as my bedroom— I looked at the spot on the dresser where our wedding picture used to be. I thought of our beach honeymoon and our regular vacations to Sanibel Island. Gene and I had loved sitting on the beach watching the sunset. We had liked being an old married couple, I'd thought. We'd even been planning a thirtieth-anniversary trip to Hawaii.

The divorce dashed any hopes of that or any other trip. The afternoon I signed the legal papers a friend called to ask how I was. "I'm five years, eleven months, and twenty-eight days till retirement," I told her. And that's what my life became: put one foot in front of the other, each day the same as the one before.

I tried to stay busy; it helped to keep my mind off things. But I only had so much energy. Eventually I had to stop and rest. Then my mind would start racing with all kinds of fantasies about what Gene and that other woman must be doing. Taking trips, probably, and watching sunsets. *I hate this!* I railed at God. *I hate what my life has become.*

Sometimes in the throes of this self-torture my mind would grow quiet, except for what seemed to be the whisper of a long-forgotten friend. *"This is not what I planned for you, Cathy. I don't want you to just get by; I want you to have an abundant life."* But could I trust that whisper? Could I ever trust again?

I had plenty of friends, and they all tried to help. They'd invite me out to dinner, have me over to munch popcorn and watch a video, and go antiquing on weekends. I appreciated their efforts, really, but my heart wasn't in it. It was all just a way of marking time till...till what?

Then a friend told me about a trip to Hilton Head, South Carolina. She had to go for her job and invited me along. "It will do you good," she insisted.

I wasn't so sure; the beach would remind me of the sunsets on Sanibel Island and of the never-to-be-taken Hawaii anniversary vacation.

But my friend wore me down. I decided to go. To my surprise, I enjoyed myself. Until one evening when a bunch of us went out to eat. "Oh, look!" someone said, pointing out the window. All of us turned our heads. And just like that I flashed back to those vacations with Gene.

"Isn't it beautiful?" one of the girls at the table asked.

"I'm not big on sunsets," I announced. *Not anymore*, I thought. On the way back to the room I prayed, *Lord, please help. I've never felt so alone in my whole life. I don't know how to do divorce.*

No wonder, then, that Valentine's Day was tough, especially this one. I moped around the house until I found myself in front of the bookcase. There, among all those self-help tomes, a dog-eared paperback titled *In His Steps* by Charles M. Sheldon caught my eye. It's the story of a minister who challenges his congregation to ask themselves "What would Jesus do?" in every situation. If you've never heard of the book, maybe you've seen a WWJD bracelet.

I cradled the book in my hands. What would Jesus do? The question seemed perfectly absurd. What, as a beaten-down divorcée, would Jesus do? Yet in the same instant it made perfect sense. There is only one answer to the question posed by those four simple words: love. I would love everything my life contained—its pain and its joy. I would love this empty house, love even my own loneliness if it came to that. Above all I would love Christ, for it is from His love that all other love comes. And someday I would love sunsets again.

Those four words became my motto. I posted them on a bulletin board in the office where I could easily see them. When the toilet overflowed and there was no husband to fix it, I said them. If I felt angry at myself for things I had given up to be married, I'd repeat those words: What would Jesus do? And anytime someone called with a juicy update on my husband's affair, I'd say those words to myself and tell the person I didn't want to hear the gossip.

Then one night a couple of months after I'd found that book, my phone rang. Gene. "I'm in the hospital," he informed me. His voice sounded weak, even a little afraid. I steeled myself against the feelings welling up. "I've been admitted for a heart problem."

I heard him out, thanked him for letting me know, and hung up.

Fine, I thought. *Let her take care of him.* But those four words on the bulletin board stared back at me: What would Jesus do? I reached up and ran my fingers across the paper. But how could I even face the man who had betrayed me?

The very words that had helped me so much now haunted me. What would Jesus do? I knew what He would do—go see Gene. So I went to the hospital. Gene looked surprised to see me. "You called me, right?" I said. "When someone calls from the hospital, you go and visit them."

We talked for a while. Doctors said he would be out soon. It wasn't as serious as he'd first feared, and my training told me he would be all right if he'd just take a little better care of himself. "I had quite a scare," he said, as if I were the only one who could have understood.

What if he hadn't made it? I asked myself. *He would have died and you would still be carrying around all that bitterness and anger.* I left Gene's hospital room that day knowing I wasn't in love with him anymore. But I had learned that I could show him love and think of him without anger or hatred—the first step toward forgiveness and healing. It made me feel incredibly strong.

Still, there was one piece of business left. I mentioned it to a woman at work. "I've always wanted to go to Hawaii," I said one day over coffee. "I just don't have anyone to go with." She looked at me in amazement. "Me too!" We started planning right then and there.

It was a long way to go for a sunset, but I knew it would be beautiful.

Come Home

God says to His children: Are you lonesome?
Breathe out My name. Come to Me and I will be
your friend. Are you sick? Come to Me for healing.
Are you left out of things? Feeling rejected and
pushed aside? Come home to Me.

ALICE CHAPIN

A Chance to Serve

BY SUZANNE M. WILLIAMS

The threat of snow hung in the air as I cruised through Harrisburg that Saturday. It was an hour past midnight. *Another hour to go*, I thought. I was due to get off my shift early. The heater in my patrol car was humming. Inside, though, I felt as cold and empty as the streets.

At one time God's purpose for my life had seemed clear. Then my marriage failed. A year after my divorce I was still struggling to get my life back on track. Even in church, where I used to feel so at home, I kept wondering, *Is there a place for me here as a divorced Christian woman?*

I began going to a new church, thinking it would be a good way to start over. But most of the activities were for families or young singles. I didn't fit in either category. *Are my days of serving You over, Lord?* I prayed. *Can You still use me?*

At least at work I didn't have to wonder about what I was doing. I didn't question my purpose. I'd been a policewoman for six years, and I was confident in my ability to do my job.

I drove north, heading uptown past abandoned, run-down houses. Through the half-open window I saw a stray cat. It eyed me suspiciously before the crackle of my police radio sent it scurrying into the shadows.

"Man down," the dispatcher's voice blared out. "Shot. 510 Woodbine Street." Only two blocks away. I flipped on the siren and rounded the corner, my adrenaline pulsing. Tires squealing, I pulled to a stop in a dark, litter-strewn alley next to the house. I was the first officer on the scene.

A teenage boy raced out the front door. "Hurry!" he yelled. "My cousin's been shot!"

I grabbed the first-aid kit from the trunk and ran inside after him. The panic and tension in the house hit me immediately. People crammed into the living room, screaming. The smells of sweat and blood filled the air. Someone was sobbing. I pushed my way through.

A young black man, maybe eighteen or nineteen, lay on the bare linoleum, bleeding profusely from the mouth. I dropped to my knees beside him. "What happened?"

"Jerome got in a fight down the street, and they came after him" someone said.

Jerome was conscious and alert. It was the dark pool of blood spreading beneath his head that scared me. I wasn't a trained paramedic. And my first-aid kit held only the basics—there was nothing to treat a serious gunshot wound.

I reached toward Jerome. He pulled away. Even though he couldn't talk, fear and distrust were written all over his face. Did he sense my uncertainty?

I shouted over the din, hoping I sounded like I knew what I was doing. "Bring a blanket and pillow! Help me take off his boots and loosen his belt!"

"Get his mom," someone shouted.

I gently propped the pillow under Jerome's knees and put the blanket over him. The crowd packed in closer. I could feel their urgency—so intense it was almost like anger—pressing down on me as I bent over Jerome. *We need the paramedics,* I thought frantically. *Now.*

A girl, barely a teenager, got right up in my face. "Do something!" Tears streaked her cheeks. "You've gotta help my brother!"

Oh, Lord, You've got to help me! I thought. *Please! What do I do now?*

I looked at Jerome again. He had closed his eyes.

Oh, no! He's going to die! I knew there was only one thing left I could do—that I must do. I laid my hand on his head and prayed. Out loud.

"Jerome, I speak life to you in the name of Jesus."

My voice was unwavering, the conviction in it surprising even me. In my years of police work I'd prayed silently many times on the way to calls. But never out loud, let alone in front of anyone else.

"You will live and not die," I said. "And you will declare the glory of the Lord. I thank You, Father, that no weapon formed against Jerome shall prosper, that no evil shall befall him."

The noise of the crowd seemed to fade as God's word poured from me.

"I thank You, Lord, that You give Your angels charge over Jerome to guard him in all his ways."

Beneath my hand, Jerome relaxed. Calm settled over the room, which had been throbbing with desperation only moments before.

Then two police officers ran in, paramedics at their heels. They took over and stabilized Jerome. As they were wheeling him to the ambulance, Jerome's cousin Mack, the young man who'd run to get me, lunged for one of the officers.

The calm exploded into panic. The crowd surged forward, swallowing up the blue uniforms of my fellow officers. I radioed for backup.

As the ambulance sped away more police arrived on the scene. They managed to get everyone except the family out of the house. Jerome's sister, Star, and I tried to console Mack, who was huddled on the floor, sobbing, convinced his cousin was dead, gone forever. Nothing we said seemed to penetrate Mack's grief.

Finally one of the adults led Mack and Star outside. I was assigned to wait in the house alone until the forensics unit showed up to photograph and process the scene.

I walked through the rooms. The furniture was shoved every which way, the linoleum marred with splotches of drying blood. I paused in front of the family pictures on the wall and stared at the photos, my gaze skipping from Jerome to his sister to a woman who looked to be their mother. *Their lives will never be the same after tonight,* I thought. *I wish I could have done more for Jerome.*

Then a small wooden plaque caught my eye. "God, grant me the serenity to accept the things I cannot change..." I read. *There is something I can do,* I decided. *I can keep praying for Jerome and his family.*

About two weeks later I got a message at the station house. Jerome's mom, Cartricia Godbee, had called looking for me. Jerome was going to be fine. He'd been in a coma, on life support, but he was out of danger. A .22-caliber bullet had lodged in his neck, missing his spinal cord and jugular vein by less than a quarter of an inch. Amazingly, it hadn't caused any permanent damage. Cartricia asked me to stop by the hospital to see them.

The next day happened to be my day off, and I went. It was wonderful to see Jerome sitting up in his bed, his family gathered around him. He had a peaceful glow on his face, so different from the fear and distrust I'd seen the night of the shooting.

Cartricia got up from his bedside and hugged me. "I heard about everything you did for my son," she said. "That night I'd asked him to go to church with me, but he went to a party instead," she explained. After church she had gone out to eat with friends. She'd had no idea what happened until she got home and saw the ambulance. "The whole ride to the hospital I was praying for Jerome, asking him to call on Jesus," she said. "I could tell he was trying, even though he couldn't talk. When people told me later that you were praying for my son too...well, I can't tell you how much that meant to me. Thank you."

I talked to Cartricia again a few days later. Jerome had been released from the hospital, and she invited me to a welcome home party for him at their church. "Would you wear your uniform and talk to the kids about the night he got shot? How you prayed?"

I got permission to appear in uniform off-duty, and several nights later I nervously stepped into Mount Calvary Church of God in Christ. In the first pew, I saw Jerome and his family—his sisters, his cousin Mack, and, of course, his mother. They all smiled, and Cartricia beckoned me to join them.

The service began. Soon my trepidation vanished, swept away by the joyous music and singing. When the reverend called me up to speak, I directed my words at the thirty or so teenagers in the back pews and talked about what had happened the night of the shooting, how I'd prayed for Jerome. "What you meet up with out on the streets is a lie," I told them. "The Lord's truth is inside you. God loves you, and He has a special plan and purpose for your life."

What about me? I wondered, stepping down and returning to my seat next to Jerome. As I bowed my head, the reverend asked if anyone would like to come forward and ask Jesus into his heart. I heard a rustle in the aisle. Then the congregation broke into cheers and thunderous applause. I looked up. Almost all the teenagers were at the altar!

I felt a rush of warmth inside. At last I understood what God wanted to show me. He still had a purpose for my life, and a place for me in His church. God only asks that I be available to serve Him. He will give me the ability and the opportunity to do it.

God's Ways

Oh, the depth of the riches both of the wisdom and knowledge of God! How unsearchable are His judgments and unfathomable His ways!

ROMANS 11:33 NASB

The Outcast

BY KAY GOLBECK

A chill ran through me. I had just been introduced to one of the inmates early in my first week as chaplain at the women's prison in Goochland, Virginia.

I tried to find something pleasant about the woman as she glared at me, but it was difficult. It was even hard to determine her age, for her face was horribly scarred and her hair was more wildcat than human.

The matron said Barbara was thirty-five, but her smouldering eyes reflected what seemed like centuries of pent-up hate.

When I hesitantly stretched out my hand to shake hers, she eyed it with contempt, glared at me for a steely second, then spun around and strode back to her cell.

"Barbara's a bad one, I'm afraid," sighed Warden Kates. "She's considered hopeless for rehabilitation. Those face scars are from knifings, and that awful skin on her neck and arm is where a bucket of lye was thrown at her in a fight. She's so vicious that none of the other prisoners here will have anything to do with her."

Warden Kates went on to tell how someone had made the mistake of sitting too close to Barbara one time in the dining hall, crowding her a bit. The adventurer leaped up screaming, blood streaming down her leg. It had been slit from ankle to knee with a stolen spoon Barbara had honed to razor sharpness on the cement floor of her cell.

I shuddered and wondered if this wasn't one prisoner I should avoid. Though I had attended Bible school and learned counseling techniques, I was fairly inexperienced and had never dealt with hardened criminals.

The next morning I heard sweeping outside my office. Through the window I saw it was Barbara. In a moment of boldness, I called out the window, "Good morning!"

She kept her head down, angrily slashing at the walk with the broom. "Ain't supposed to talk to no one while I'm workin'!" she snarled.

Forcing myself to continue, I said, "Well, I'll come to your cottage when you're finished."

"Forget it!" she snapped. "Nothin' to talk about." Then she was gone.

It's just as well, I thought. I didn't know how to talk to someone like that. Maybe I had better leave well enough alone. All I could do, I felt, was to pray for her.

Yet something kept drawing me back to this sullen prisoner.

A few days later I found myself looking up her record. As I read through the thick folder, I could well understand why everyone felt Barbara was hopeless. I learned that she was now in prison for larceny. Because it was her third conviction, ten additional years—"Come-back time," the girls call it—had been added to her basic sentence. Each of Barbara's former confinements in prisons around the state was documented with page after page of punishment reports for fighting, stealing, brewing "hooch," and assaulting guards. I also noted that Barbara had no family on the outside. Her parents had disappeared when she was very young. After a succession of foster homes, there had been a stormy marriage that had ended in divorce. In all of her folder, I failed to find one constructive element on which I could try to build a relationship.

"How does Barbara get along with the other girls?" I asked the matron of her cottage.

"Oh, she's hopeless!" she snorted. "There's no good in her at all. We just leave her alone and keep out of her way. It's a lot safer."

When I suggested that we might pray for Barbara, the matron laughed. "Me? Pray for that one? You won't catch me wasting my prayers on the likes of her!"

As I left the building, I felt my stubbornness flare. If the matron wouldn't help, I'd redouble my own prayers. Besides, wasn't Barbara the lost sheep that Jesus talked about, the one out of a hundred for whom we had to search through the rocky hills?

The next day I had a counseling session with Barbara. She sat in a chair by my desk like a trapped animal, head down, eyes darting toward the door.

Summoning up all my spiritual convictions and counseling training, I tried to reach this lonely soul trapped within the scarred, tormented body.

"Barbara, do you know that God loves you?"

"Ain't nobody loves me!" Her hands twisted together in her lap.

"Jesus gave His life for us so that we can start new lives for ourselves."

She spat on the floor and looked up at me, glaring. "Don't want none of that preachin' stuff. It's all words...don't mean a thing!" She got up and headed for the door.

A few times after that I'd try to speak to her while she was doing chores. But she would keep her head down as she swept or would glare at me in hate. Discouraged, I found myself beginning to avoid her. I justified this with the thought that some people really are hopeless. "Lord," I sighed, "I give up. I leave her to You."

But though I stayed away from Barbara, something I had seen deep in those dark eyes continued to haunt me.

I joined the prisoners out on the lawn one hot summer day during recreation time. Then I noticed Barbara. As usual she was standing apart from the others. The heat felt like a blanket, and I thought how readily my pale Canadian skin burned in this fierce southern sun. The other girls were strolling and talking, but Barbara stood alone, motionless. As I looked at her, my eyes were drawn to her scarred throat, bare where the collar of her blouse was turned back. Her skin there looked so thin and tightly drawn.

Oh, I thought, *how that poor skin must burn when she gets too much sun on it. It looks so sensitive....*

Suddenly I remembered that somewhere in my belongings was a soft pink silk handkerchief. Back in my room I rummaged until I found it, along with two gold-colored pins. I hesitated. Then I forced myself to walk casually outside toward Barbara.

When she saw me coming, it took all my determination to keep going in her direction. I could see the anger seething in her dark eyes. The matron's words echoed in my memory: *We keep out of her way. It's a lot safer.*

"Barbara," I said, my voice trembling in spite of myself, "this sun is burning me up. And your neck looks so sensitive. Would you let me pin this little piece of silk on the neckline of your blouse to protect you from the sun?"

My words sounded foolish to me. They must have sounded strange to Barbara too, judging from her look of confusion. But I tried to ignore her clenched fists as I held out the little pink square of silk. Silently praying for courage, I took the final step, reached, up and laid the tiny handkerchief across her throat. With fumbling fingers I fastened it in place with the pins.

Barbara said nothing, but two tears welled up in her dark eyes to run down her scarred cheeks and moisten the square of pink. Except for that, her face was as stony as ever. She stamped her foot, gritted her teeth, and, knuckling her tears away, spat on the ground.

I turned away from her and sought the shelter of my office. Had I made any contact? I wondered. Was this a beginning? A Scripture buried in my memory reminded me that when God begins a work, He can be counted on to finish it. I kept praying, "Lord, don't let me scare her off now. Please guide me by Your Spirit."

A few days later I was prompted to contact Barbara again. This time, as she sat in my office, I didn't try to lead her into the plan of salvation. I just told her that I wanted to be her friend.

She glanced at me warily. "Why?"

I didn't have the words to answer. Then I remembered my own loneliness, growing up in a family of younger sisters and brothers who seemed so much more attractive and accomplished than I was. I reached out to touch Barbara's hand then thought better of it. I just said, "Because I know how it is to have no friends."

For an instant a spark of understanding flickered in her eyes.

As the months went by, I kept trying to get through to Barbara. Sometimes she would seem receptive. We talked of our lives, disappointments, and hopes. I told her how I had been confined to bed for eight years with arthritis that was considered incurable.

"How come you got better?"

"Jesus...the Lord Jesus healed me."

Then at our next meeting she would be gone again, retreating into herself like an animal burrowing into the corner of its cage.

But I kept trying to let Barbara know in little ways that she was loved.

Then one morning her matron gave me a note. It was tear-splotched, the crude spelling all but indecipherable. But as nearly as I could tell, the note said, "Chaplain, I ain't slept all night. You better get down here right away."

I ran to Barbara's cell. She was lying on her cot, staring at the ceiling with eyes red and swollen. When I entered the room, she flung herself at me and burst into sobbing that shook her whole frame. I hugged her, praying, rejoicing because I knew what had happened. Through the months, the gentle urging of His Spirit had finally penetrated Barbara's heart. She had opened the door and let Him in. The vicious, hardened criminal had died. In its place was a new creature, awash with God's love. The little square of pink silk was pinned to her pillow.

From then on Barbara was a different person. Not only were her chores done quickly and efficiently, but she began searching for educational courses to take in her free time. "I know I don't speak too good," she confessed to me.

She spent a lot of time reading the Bible and helped me in little ways.

Months later, completely rehabilitated, she was released, a poised, alert, almost handsome woman. Later I found myself filling out recommendations for her for Bible schools then for jobs in nursing homes. Eventually, she became a county supervisor of all the nursing homes for the elderly in a large midwestern state.

Recently, I opened one of my friend Barbara's letters. Inside was a photo of Barbara, her lye-scarred arms holding a tiny elderly lady with a halo of white hair around a wrinkled face glowing with joy.

"This little old lady had no faith or hope," wrote Barbara, "but now she does. She's looking to Jesus for all her needs, just as I keep looking to Him for all of mine."

My tears moistened the letter, and my heart felt as if it would burst with joy. If God could use a little scrap of silk to begin such a transformation in a hopeless person, then surely there is hope for all the world.

Transforming Grace

For [God] is, indeed, a wonderful Father
who longs to pour out His mercy upon us,
and whose majesty is so great that He
can transform us from deep within.

TERESA OF AVILA

The Swill Gang

BY PATRICIA LORENZ

A friend loves at all times" (Proverbs 17:7 NIV)

I'd closed the curtains in my family room, flipped through the TV channels, and settled into my green rocker for another night alone when the phone rang. It was a woman named Sunny calling from Valdosta, Georgia.

"I just read something you wrote in *The Single Parent* magazine and I have to talk to you. I'm a single parent too, and sometimes I just don't know if I can make it on my own. I thought it would help to talk to someone else who's raising children alone." We talked for an hour that night, and then Sunny called every couple of weeks.

A few months later Sunny told me she wanted to move back north, so I invited her to Milwaukee for a weekend to attend a conference for single people. She stayed for a week and bought a house while she was here. She kept calling me her best friend even though I was wallowing too deep in my own miseries to be anybody's best anything. That year was the worst of my life, and I just was not up to helping someone else solve her problems.

In fact, I needed someone who would listen to my own problems. And they were many. The man I'd dated for ten months suddenly moved to Oklahoma to start a new career. My ex-husband died of leukemia, not long after he had married his girlfriend on the day our divorce was final. Our nine-year-old son, Andrew, was devastated by his father's death, but I was too angry about the whole divorce thing in the first place even to know how to grieve.

That same year my twenty-year-old daughter, Jeanne, got caught in the middle of the California earthquake, and I lived through nightmarish days until I learned she was safe. And my eighteen-year-old daughter, Julie, after graduating from high school, decided to spend the summer before college testing my sense of "loving motherhood." We hollered at and bickered with each other all summer.

I wondered if I just couldn't get used to the idea of first Harold, then Jeanne, and now Julie leaving me. Many nights my family room felt like an empty auditorium as I sat alone with the TV set. *Lord,* I wondered, *what has happened to my family? Will this room ever seem full again?*

Then, as a favor to Sunny, after she made the move to Milwaukee with her two young daughters, I decided to gather some of my women friends to meet her. I called every woman I knew—friends from church, work, and the neighborhood. Friends I met over the years through other people. Mothers of my children's friends. One from my writing club.

I was a bit nervous at first, inviting them to my house all at once, knowing that few of them knew one another. When they arrived I introduced everyone; and before long we were talking, laughing, and gabbing like old friends about our jobs, children, and lifestyles. Sunny was delighted. In fact, she said, "You people are downright interesting!"

Tina piped up, "I think we should do this every month! It can be our club. We could call it the Southeastern Wisconsin Interesting Ladies League! S-W-I-L-L."

I laughed. "SWILL! SWILL? We're going to form a club and call it SWILL?"

"Why not?" Sharon asked. "We can gather together, unload all the swill that creeps into our lives, and get support from one another."

So it began. We decided to meet at my house every month since I have the largest family room and the fewest family members to uproot on Friday nights.

We kept it simple. SWILL would have only one rule—confidentiality. Whatever problems or heartaches were discussed in that family room during our SWILL meetings would stay in that room. We would trust one another, care about one another, and help one another if possible.

During the past three years at least twenty-five women have woven their way in and out of the SWILL meetings. Anyone can bring an interesting friend to the meetings, and if that friend likes us she can become a regular. Sometimes we've had a dozen at one time, and other months, because of hectic schedules, we've had only three or four.

As we got to know each other, we began to care more and more about one another. We became a family. I never worry about cleaning the house before a SWILL meeting because nobody's there to do a white glove inspection. And I don't worry about fancy refreshments. If one of us is having a chocolate or salty foods craving, she brings a bag of candy or pretzels to toss on the coffee table to share. We resolved from the beginning never to get bogged down, as some clubs do, with a fancy food complex.

SWILL welcomes everyone regardless of age, race, religion, or occupation. Everyone from Carrie, a young married woman in her late twenties with four small children, struggling with the possibility of her marriage ending, to Eunice, who's been married for forty-two years and taken enough college-level classes in her retirement to be one of the most interesting people in the group.

When one of our group, Linda, died of heart failure at age thirty-nine after meeting with us only a short time, we mourned together. Later we discussed ways to solve the medical insurance problems that often face single, overstressed parents like Linda, who had worked as many as three jobs to make ends meet.

When Jody's teenage son Daniel died in a car accident, we held one another and cried with Jody at the funeral.

When Gail, whose children were starting college, went back to school to study nursing, we spent hours talking her into staying in school when she wanted to quit. One of our members, a counselor, helped Gail through some test anxiety problems one night. Gail graduated in May and we all took a bow.

When Barb's son came home from Desert Storm, he moved back in to her and her husband's "empty nest." Then a few months later her daughter moved back home with her husband and new baby. We listened to the ups and downs of Barb's five-adults-in-one-house, three-generation family. We gave her lots of advice, including the fact that it was okay for her to go back to work full time.

Carol, whose happy marriage rubs off on all of us, points out that even a happy marriage isn't perfect all the time, but that a sense of humor can get you through most of the swill that marriage can dish out.

Sunny benefited tremendously from SWILL. She became more independent; found a wonderful job in the Milwaukee school system; made lots of new friends at work, in her neighborhood, and in her church; and moved on to start her own support network.

What did SWILL do for me, the one who was simply trying to find a few friends for Sunny? I think I'm the one who benefited most. These women—single, separated, divorced, married, from all walks of life—opened their hearts and their lives to me, month after month. They listened to me, laughed with me, and helped me through the rough times of being a single parent.

Now that I have three children in college at once and a twelve-year-old at home, they help me even more through the struggles by offering financial advice as well as emotional help. I've learned to talk about my fears and my failures. I've learned to admit that I'm scared at times and that it's okay to have conflicts with the ones you love.

I've also learned how important it is to get out of the house and get plenty of exercise. Gail and I started roller-skating two or three times a week on the bike path near Lake Michigan. And Betsy (another SWILL member) and I fast-walk every Saturday morning for an hour.

One thing's for sure—the last three years have been some of my best because of the interesting and loving women friends I made through SWILL. As for this year, well, I'm just wondering if we shouldn't change our name to SWELL. Because we are. A swell bunch of women who, during the past three years, have become a family to one another, a nonjudgmental support system that's always there on the first Friday of each month.

Once again the good Lord has filled my family room with "family"—a new family of friends. It's amazing how much love I feel now that I've learned to open up my life to these friends and to nourish that friendship on a regular basis.

Be There

Let us consider how to stir up one another to love and good works, not neglecting to meet together...but encouraging one another.

HEBREWS 10:24–25 ESV

A Nurse Named Tami

BY ALINE NEWMAN

I adjusted the blinds to let the sunshine into Becky's room at Memorial Sloan-Kettering Cancer Center. It was one of those luminous late summer days in Manhattan when the sidewalks are thick with people—office workers, shoppers, vendors, and tourists from all over the world. The energy was almost palpable, not at all like the quiet little town where I lived in Upstate where everyone knew everyone else.

"Come and look," I said to Becky and her mom, my sister Kathy. "It's an amazing view."

My nineteen-year-old niece had been battling Hodgkin's disease, a form of cancer, since January. She'd entered Sloan-Kettering that morning so she could have a stem cell transplant, a desperate effort to wipe out the cancer that radiation and chemotherapy hadn't been able to destroy. It had been a long, tough year, and I just wanted this procedure to cure Becky and for things to go back to normal.

I was still admiring the view when the door opened and in waltzed a young woman. Not just any young woman. This one had spiky black hair, a line of earrings snaking down each ear, eyebrow rings, and a stud in her nose. The silver glinted in the sunlight, and for a moment I just stared. "May I help you?" I asked.

"Hi, I'm Tami. I'm going to be Becky's primary care nurse." Becky sat up and shook Tami's hand. I tore my eyes from Tami's face long enough to glance at her uniform. Something told me a belly button ring lurked underneath it. I'd seen a few kids decked out like this when I was substitute teaching, but they were a tiny minority in our town. With two teenage sons, I'd seen my share of music videos. But this girl was a hospital nurse! How could someone who seemed to have no problem inflicting damage on her own body be trusted to take care of someone else's?

I watched silently as Tami hooked up Becky to a couple of monitors. "I'll be back to check on you later," she said.

Becky turned to me the moment Tami left the room. "Aunt Ine, how could you act like that? She'll think you don't like her!"

"What? I didn't say anything."

"You didn't have to. The look on your face said it all." I'd never been very good at hiding my feelings. But I had to watch out for Becky. My only niece was in a fight for her life. She needed someone caring, dependable, and responsible as her nurse.

I unpacked Becky's things and said nothing, resolving to keep an eye on Tami. No point in upsetting Becky further. She'd been through so much already, having to drop out of college her freshman year. Nine months of outpatient treatment at Sloan-Kettering. And the worst symptom of her illness—an intense itching that made it almost impossible for her to sleep. Her only relief was having someone rub her feet, where the itching was most severe. Becky's father had to stay Upstate and work, so I often made the eight-hour trip to Manhattan to help my sister with the round-the-clock foot rubs while Becky was being treated.

My prayers had become round-the-clock too. Ever since her diagnosis Becky had been optimistic, a real fighter. "My grandfather lived for years after he got sick," she told her doctor. "I'm going to be just like him." But every time it seemed Becky was getting better, we got more bad news. My pleas turned into frantic questions: *Why aren't You helping Becky, God? Why aren't You watching over her?*

We couldn't even rub Becky's feet anymore without wearing gowns, masks, and gloves because she was at a high risk for infection until she got her new stem cells. Her friends couldn't visit her. But Becky's face lit up whenever Tami came in. They chattered on about TV shows, music, boys—especially their exes. It was like they'd known each other for years! How could my wholesome niece—who loved the outdoors and never bothered with jewelry—be so comfortable with a big-city girl who had more metal on her than a bicycle chain? Granted, some days Tami looked almost normal—the piercings were visible but the silver was missing.

One afternoon she strutted in wearing a leather dog collar studded with metal spikes. "That girl has a problem," I told Becky after Tami left. "Nobody with a healthy self-image would dress like that."

Becky rolled her eyes. "It doesn't mean anything, Aunt Ine. It's just her style!"

Style? I didn't see anything stylish about it. But I had to admit I also couldn't see any reason to doubt Tami's nursing skills. In fact, Becky seemed so at ease with Tami that Kathy and I started going for walks while she was on duty. The day of Becky's stem cell transplant, we went all the way to South Street Seaport to buy her a watch for her "transplant birthday."

Becky recovered quickly, and on Halloween she was released. "I'll miss you, Becky," Tami said as she hugged her good-bye, her eyes moistening. "Now go home and celebrate."

The celebration didn't last. Right after Thanksgiving the cancer came back. Becky started outpatient radiation treatments again. Then she caught a cold she couldn't shake. The day after Christmas she was rushed back to Sloan-Kettering. She had pneumonia.

A couple of days later I sat alone in the waiting room reading the same magazine paragraph over and over while I waited for Becky to be brought out. Someone sat down in the chair next to me. Tami. There was something almost comforting about her familiar strangeness. She looked me straight in the eye. "You know Becky's in very bad shape," she said. "There's someone I think she needs to speak to."

"Who?"

"Her old boyfriend. Can you track him down?" Before I could answer, Tami slipped a piece of paper into my hand. "My home phone number," she explained. "In case you ever need me." With that she hurried off on her rounds. For a moment I felt as dumbfounded as I'd been the first time I'd seen Tami. I tucked her number into my purse and went to find Kathy so we could contact Becky's ex.

Tami was right. Becky was in good spirits after she talked to her old boyfriend. But her lungs were filling up with fluid and she developed shingles.

By December 30 the worst seemed over. Becky had even improved enough to eat a Big Mac. On New Year's Eve morning, I told Kathy to catch up on her sleep. I planned to sit with Becky a few hours before taking the train home to spend the holiday with my husband and sons. I couldn't wait for the year to end. I wanted to forget the previous year.

But it wasn't over yet. Becky's doctor had ordered an X-ray that morning. The results came back just as my sister arrived at the hospital. The moment I saw the doctor, I started shaking.

"The cancer has exploded inside Becky's chest," she said.

"What do you mean?"

The doctor shook her head. "It means the cancer will grow into Becky's throat. When it does, she won't be able to breathe." Her voice sank to a whisper. "You'd better call the rest of the family—now."

Within an hour the others were on their way. But they wouldn't get to the city until at least midnight. Somehow we'd have to get through the night on our own. We couldn't tell Becky, not when she was finally feeling better. Not on New Year's Eve.

Kathy sat with Becky. But I couldn't. One look at my face and Becky would see my feelings as clear as always. So I paced. Around and around the halls I went, trying to rid my mind of the image of Becky gasping for air. My niece was dying. And I couldn't stop it. Couldn't even manage to sit with her and rub her feet.

Every prayer I'd said for Becky had failed, yet I could do nothing else but pray. *Oh, God, just take care of my niece. Give her comfort. Help me understand all this!*

Down the hall a nurse turned the corner. I wished it had been Tami, but she was off for the holiday. I dug into my purse and pulled out her number. *In case you ever need me.* I hesitated. It was New Year's Eve after all, and Tami was young and single. Finally I went to a phone and called her. "If you could maybe come keep Becky company for just an hour...give us time to gather our senses..."

"Think you can hold on till eight o'clock?"

"Oh, yes! I know you probably already have plans."

"I do now. See you soon," she said.

I pulled myself together and joined my sister in Becky's room.

Right at 8:00 p.m. Tami burst in, eyes shining. Hoisting a bottle of sparkling grape juice into the air, she shouted, "Let's party!"

Tami unloaded a stack of videos, four pints of Ben & Jerry's ice cream, and four plastic champagne glasses on the windowsill. In minutes we were all scrunched together on the bed watching movies, eating ice cream, and toasting with grape juice. We were laughing so much we hardly noticed when midnight passed. Who knew someone who'd once seemed so strange to me could make things feel so normal? I watched Tami slip her hand—a ring on nearly every finger—into Becky's. "Judge not according to the appearance," I recalled from the Bible. Tami was the answer to prayer I'd been waiting for. She hadn't looked like the answer I'd wanted. Yet God had provided in His own perfect way. He had provided for me by providing for Becky.

Tami would be there again four weeks later when Becky slipped away peacefully, surrounded by all of us who loved her. When I think of Tami—and that's often—I think of the joy she brought to those final minutes of a terrible year. And the only thing I remember about how she looked that night is the love in her eyes.

Through the Eyes of Love

God looks at the world through the eyes of love.
If we, therefore, as human beings made in the image
of God also want to see reality...as it truly is, then we,
too, must learn to look at what we see with love.

ROBERTA BONDI

Words of Love

BY LACHANZE

D*ear God, why did this happen? I've always tried to live a good life, to follow Your will. Why have You left me without the father of my children? Why did You take Calvin? How could You? What am I to do now?*

I shut my journal and closed my eyes. My young daughters, Celia and Zaya, were both asleep. The apartment was eerily quiet, like a theater after the show has ended and the set struck. My husband, a trader at Cantor Fitzgerald, had been killed six months earlier on 9/11 in the World Trade Center attack.

During the days, there were visits from family and condolences from friends, colleagues, even strangers. There were the inevitable media interviews. But at night there were just my girls without their father to read them a bedtime story and me without a husband to hold. I thought I'd earned my happily-ever-after when Calvin and I had gotten married. Why had God taken it all away?

My name, LaChanze, means "one who is charmed" in Creole. If you had seen my family right before that day in 2001, you might have thought it fitting. My life before that had been far from easy. My parents were teens when they had me in Florida.

Dad was in the Coast Guard, and Mom worked various jobs to help make ends meet.

Then my parents divorced when I was ten. Suddenly, I had to grow up. I had lots of responsibilities. I'd clean up and help Mom make breakfast for my little brothers. I'd babysit while Mom was at work. Whenever I had a moment to myself, I'd write in the journal Mom had given me, sometimes about things that had happened at school or home. But more about things I wanted to happen, like traveling the world or becoming an actress.

Ever since Mom had taken me to see the show *Chicago*, I'd wanted nothing more than to be up onstage making people feel the way I did at the show—filled with wonder and joy. All my journal entries ended with a prayer for God to help or teach me. I'd ask Him to prepare me for whatever was to come. Often it was just, "Thy will, Lord, not mine." I wanted to trust God with all my heart, to trust His plan for my future.

My mom remarried and we settled in Connecticut. I went to a tough high school but stuck close to my theater friends. If I got lonely, I turned to my journal, rereading past entries to recognize God's blessings and how He'd guided me, like a road map of my life.

I went to the University of the Arts in Philadelphia and majored in theater and dance. Then the movie *The Color Purple* came out with Whoopi Goldberg in the lead role of Celie. I was blown away by this story of a girl who overcame adversity to learn to love herself. I felt a special connection with her because she too kept a journal in which she wrote to God. Instantly, the movie became my favorite.

Things were starting to come together in my own life. I worked as a tap dancer in Atlantic City one summer on a show called *Uptown...It's Hot!* It ended up on Broadway. Theater work came fairly steadily after that. I got my big break in *Once on This Island*. I earned a Tony nomination. I wasn't disappointed not to win. Just to be nominated was the thrill of my life! The only thing missing was someone to share my life with.

One Memorial Day weekend, I was at a restaurant with a friend when a handsome man introduced himself as Calvin Gooding and started chatting with us. Later, I bumped into him near the restrooms.

"I'd like to call you sometime," he said. "Take you out for dinner, ice cream, a trip to the moon—whatever you want." He called me that same night. Eight months later we were engaged.

We went to Los Angeles for a year so I could take a lead role in the musical *Ragtime*. Calvin had no problem adjusting—he drew people to him like a magnet. I loved to see him pull up to the theater in his convertible to pick me up after a matinee, his smile flashing.

Back in New York, we married. I was pregnant before our first anniversary. Our daughter Celia was a toddler and I was eight months pregnant by September 2001. It was a happy, busy time and my journal entries were full of hope and gratitude for the future Calvin and I were building together.

In one morning, all of that disappeared. No warning. No reason. No chance to say good-bye. In my journal I wrote, *9/11/01. Calvin died today.* I couldn't bear to write more. Even seeing it in black and white didn't make it real to me. I kept feeling like Calvin was just held up at the office, that any moment he would walk through the door and scoop Celia up in his arms.

Even after his memorial service, where 1,100 people came to remember him—even then, I couldn't quite believe it. I just wanted to go home and sleep until Calvin climbed into bed beside me again.

Then my daughter Zaya came into the world. She didn't know what had happened. She only knew that she needed to be fed, changed, and held. So I pushed myself daily, doing what I needed to, to take care of my girls. I barely had time to think. For that I was thankful.

"This is part of God's plan," friends would say to comfort me.

"Don't you dare tell me that God wanted me to be alone with two small children!" I'd yell back.

I had no idea I could feel so much anger. Especially at God. I'd always been faithful and now I felt abandoned. No, betrayed by God.

Now, six months after Calvin's death, in the emptiness of the night, I demanded answers in my journal. All I got was silence. I got out of bed and went to check on my daughters. In the soft glow of the nightlight, I watched Zaya sleep. So peaceful. So completely without anger or worry or sadness. Back in my room,

I opened up my journal again and wrote: *Zaya is so beautiful and you're not here to see her. Why did you leave us, Calvin? I miss you so much.*

I couldn't bear to go to our church anymore. Memories were too painful. Celia had been christened there. Calvin and I had spent many Sundays there thanking God. God had always felt so present to me there. I had given Calvin's eulogy there.

I stopped writing in my journal. There didn't seem to be anything left to say. I was worried about money but didn't have the energy to find work. Then, out of the blue, I got a call from a playwright who'd heard about my situation. She knew my work. "I'd love for you to be in my play. You don't have to move—just sit in a chair and read monologues. It will do you good."

She was right. Becoming someone else in the theater was a welcome break from my life. I could focus my energy on something besides my grief and the stress of caring for the girls, if only for a few hours.

One night after a show, I tucked my girls in but was still wound up. I pulled out my journal and flipped to that last angry, desperate entry. *Has it really been that long?* Somehow I'd made it to a year since Calvin's death. I'd survived what had felt so unsurvivable. I started to document what was going on in my life at the moment. The show. The kids. How hard 9/11 still was to talk about. At the end of the entry I hesitated. My anger had cooled a bit, but it was still there. *Dear God*, I wrote, *please help me to forgive. Take my hand. Guide me in a new life. Amen.*

I wanted to give something back to the law firm that had helped me settle Calvin's affairs pro bono. I commissioned a painting from Derek Fordjour, an artist in Atlanta. In order to do the painting, he asked me about 9/11. I found I didn't mind telling him. Starting to journal again had made me stronger, and he was such a good listener. I found myself calling him often. I wrote about our conversations in my journals.

Then I got some incredible news I couldn't wait to tell Derek. I was cast as Celie in a new musical production of *The Color Purple*, in Atlanta. My dream role. A part of me couldn't believe I was playing it. Just like part of me couldn't believe I'd found love again. Derek and I got married. I keep a box of Calvin's things for the girls so they can know as much as possible about their dad.

The Color Purple opened on Broadway and I had the honor of portraying Celie. Each night when I was onstage living Celie's journey, I felt I was reliving my own. I knew the audience was cheering, not for me but for God working through me. He turned my pain and struggle into something beautiful.

I was and still am filled with wonder at God. Like Celie, I believe He's inside me and all around me. So each night I say a prayer: "All glory to You, dear God."

I still end my journal entries with prayers, though I tend to write only on special occasions now. I want to make sure I document the joys in life. Recently, I bought more journals. I believe there are many entries yet to come.

A Crown of Beauty

The time of the LORD's favor has come.... He will give a crown of beauty for ashes, a joyous blessing instead of mourning, festive praise instead of despair.... They will be like great oaks that the LORD has planted for his own glory.

ISAIAH 61:2-3 NLT

Not My Type

"Maybe this one will be the one," my friend Laureen said, pulling a white blouse out of my bedroom closet.

I shot her a look. Why did she have to make a big deal about tonight? Yes, I was going to a Bruce Springsteen concert with Erick, a guy I had met at a party a few years ago, but only because another friend had bailed at the last minute.

"I told you, I'm not interested in this guy," I insisted. "It's not a date. I just couldn't find anyone else to go with me."

Laureen laughed. "I wasn't talking about the guy, I was talking about the blouse."

My cheeks went red. "Oh," I said sheepishly. I was so used to friends trying to set me up that sometimes I could get a bit defensive.

The truth was, I wished I were going on a date. I was thirty-nine years old and for years I'd been praying to meet the man of my dreams who would say those three little words that would change everything: I love you.

I had been on plenty of dates over the years, and the longer I dated the more I feared that finding love was hopeless. Was my perfect man—tall and clean cut, charming and romantic, with a good job, a taste for fine dining, and a love of long walks on the beach—just an idealized fantasy? What about all those dashing guys in the photos posted on the walls of the hair salon where I worked? They seemed to mock me with their good looks and sincere gazes. All my Prince Charmings turned out to be frogs.

From what I remembered, Erick didn't fit the bill either. I'd forgotten about him until our mutual friend told me he was a Springsteen fan and might like to go to the show. At the party three years ago he'd looked like a tough guy, wearing an old white T-shirt and faded jeans. He told me he was a tugboat captain from Brooklyn.

"What can I possibly have in common with a tugboat captain?" I asked Laureen, putting on the blouse.

Laureen let out a sigh. "He could be a great guy," she said. "Give him a chance. C'mon Noreen, put your glasses on."

I laughed. Laureen always used that expression whenever she thought I was focusing on the wrong things. *God,* I prayed, taking one last glance in the mirror and tugging a few strands of hair into place, *am I really being too picky? Do You really expect me to settle for less?*

I grabbed a taxi to the arena. As the cab pulled to the curb, I peered out the window at the entrance where we agreed to meet. Erick was there all right, leaning against a lamppost. In old tattered jeans and a black Harley Davidson T-shirt with the sleeves ripped off. He featured tattoos on both arms. *Here we go,* I thought. What did I expect of a tugboat captain?

But Eric smiled sweetly when he saw me step out of the cab. "Thank you so much for this; I'm a huge Springsteen fan," he said. He fished in his pocket and pulled out the money for the ticket. "I wanted to make sure to give you this before I forgot."

It was more than he owed me, and I didn't have any change, but he said not to worry about it. *Well, at least he's not a cheapskate,* I thought.

When we got to the concert, he held the door open for me and we went inside.

The concert was great. We danced in the aisles, shouted out requests for our favorite songs ("Rosalita" and "Born to Run"), and screamed our lungs out for an encore. When it was over I didn't feel like calling it a night. Neither did Erick.

"Let's go out for a bit," he suggested. The arena lights came up and once again I could make out his enormous tattoos. *As long as we don't bump into anyone I know.*

We sat down in a restaurant. Erick caught me staring at his arms. "Do you like them?" he asked.

"Why'd you get all those?" I replied, a little taken aback by my own frankness.

"They all have different meanings," Erick said. "This one"— he pointed at a tattoo of a heart with a guitar through it—"is for my older brother. He died in an accident on the boat when he was twenty-three. We were real close." Was that a tear in his eye? A big tough tugboat captain? I reached across the table and touched his hand. Suddenly, those tattoos didn't make him seem like such a tough guy after all.

He drove me to my apartment; we sang Bruce Springsteen all the way. Erick came around to open the door for me. Then he leaned in to kiss me on the cheek.

Instinctively, I pulled away. His face fell. He looked hurt. Then Erick forced a smile. I held out my hand and he took it in his. "Good night," he said, again in that unexpectedly sweet way.

As I watched him drive away, I had to admit it had been fun. But that was it. I knew the man I was looking for. I had the perfect picture in my head, and Erick just wasn't the one. *Nice try, Lord.*

The next day, however, I made sure to call Erick and thank him for a great evening. Just because I wasn't interested didn't mean I couldn't be polite. "I never gave you back your change for the ticket," I said.

Erick laughed. "Why don't you buy me a hot dog on Saturday and we'll call it even. I know a place."

"Okay, sure," I agreed, though a hot dog was not exactly my idea of fine dining.

That weekend he took me to his favorite hot dog place—Yankee Stadium. "I love the Yankees!" I exclaimed giddily when I found out where we were going. Erick bought seats right behind home plate. "If I didn't know any better, I'd think you were trying to impress me," I said.

"Is it working?" he asked with a wink. I laughed. Well, maybe we could be friends...

Weeks passed. We saw each other again. And again. One Saturday afternoon Erick invited me down to the docks. We walked past enormous, gleaming cruise ships and charming little schooners with polished teak accents. Then Erick pointed out his tugboat. *Oh my.* It was tiny. Ropes and rust were everywhere. It certainly didn't look like much, not next to the competition.

"You wouldn't believe what she can do," Erick said, probably sensing my shock. He flipped a few switches and took the wheel. "You see that big cruise ship? This little tug can maneuver it into the exact spot it has to go. She may not look impressive, but she's as tough and dependable as any vessel around. That big ship's not going anywhere without us." I never thought about how important a tugboat was...and how deceiving looks can be.

A few weeks later he invited me over for dinner.

"How sweet," Laureen said.

"Yeah, but what will a tugboat captain cook? A can of Dinty Moore stew?" I joked. But suddenly I felt hot with shame.

Candlelight flickered and soft jazz drifted through the house. Fresh red roses were bunched in a vase on the table. Erick emerged from the kitchen carrying a platter full of piping hot Cornish game hens, garnished with greens.

"Oh, Erick, it's so lovely," I said.

"I just want to make you happy," he said. I fumbled for something to say and felt myself blushing. Finally, I looked up. His eyes met mine. This time, when he leaned in to kiss me, I didn't pull away.

We started dating regularly. Each time I learned something new about him. One day I was going on about art, trying to remember the name of a statue. "'The Thinker,'" by Rodin," he said.

"Of course, how'd you know?" I asked.

"I'm not that stupid," he said, winking at me. "Do you know your IQ?"

"Sure," I lied, "two hundred."

He laughed. "Noreen, not even Einstein had a two hundred."

Time seemed to stand still for us. *The way it does,* I thought, *for people in love.* In love? Is that what I heard myself say?

The night before Erick left on a two-week shift on the boat we stood arm-in-arm in his yard. He pointed out the constellations in the evening sky. Suddenly he turned. "I love you," he said. My heart beat wildly. There were those three little words I'd been longing to hear from the right man. But fear gripped me. My whole life, I'd pictured some other kind of Prince Charming. Was Erick the right one? I hugged him tightly, but I couldn't say a thing.

The next day, I was home alone, stirring some sauce in the kitchen, wishing I were cooking for Erick too. In the quiet apartment, I needed to hear his laugh. At work I found myself daydreaming in the middle of cutting a client's hair because I couldn't stop thinking of Erick's cute wink, the way he kept surprising me, and the way he made me feel when we were together. Was it possible that God had bigger dreams for me than I had for myself? Love was a lot more than those glossy photos on the salon wall. More than even the best we can picture for ourselves.

I counted the days until Erick came home, the way women did in the old days, when men went to sea for years. Finally, he was back on land and headed to my apartment. My hands shook as I fixed my hair. *Please God, don't let me ruin this chance,* I prayed.

I ran to open the door. "I have something to tell you," I began. I felt myself falter then just blurted, "I love you too." And all at once I realized that what was going to change my life was not hearing those three words, but saying them.

"I knew you did," Erick said.

Later, on a trip to Italy, Erick took me in his arms while we stood on the famous *Romeo and Juliet* Balcony in Verona and asked me to marry him. A true romantic as I had always dreamed. I didn't hesitate to say yes. I had asked God to send me a Prince Charming, but He gave me a Captain Erick instead. He wasn't what I had imagined; he was so much more.

True Romance

*I think true love is never blind
But rather brings an added light,
An inner vision quick to find
The beauties hid from common sight*

PHOEBE CARY

Dream Big!

BY DIANE SAWYER,
ANCHOR OF ABC WORLD NEWS

M any of us, I think, can look back and recall certain specific moments in our lives that take on greater importance the longer we live. "The past has a different pattern," T. S. Eliot wrote, "when viewed from each of our changing perspectives."

For me, one of those moments occurred when I was seventeen years old. I was a high school senior in Louisville, Kentucky, representing my state in the 1963 America's Junior Miss competition in Mobile, Alabama. Along with the other young contestants, I was doing my best to hold up under the grueling week-long schedule of interviews, agonies over hair that curled or wouldn't, photo sessions, nervous jitters, and rehearsals. In the midst of it all, there was one person who stood at the center—at least my psychological center—someone I viewed as an island in an ocean of anxiety.

She was one of the judges, a well-known writer. A woman whose sea-gray eyes fixed on you with laser penetration, whose words were always deliberate. She felt the right words could make all the difference. Her name was Catherine Marshall.

From the first moment I met Catherine Marshall, I was aware that she was holding me—indeed all of us—to a more exacting standard. While other pageant judges asked questions about favorite hobbies and social pitfalls, she sought to challenge. She felt even seventeen-year-old girls—perhaps especially seventeen-year-old girls—should be made to examine their ambitions and relate them to their values.

During the rehearsal on the last day of the pageant, the afternoon before it would all end, several of us were waiting backstage when a pageant official said Catherine Marshall wanted to speak with us. We gathered around. Most of us were expecting a last-minute pep talk or the ritual good luck wish or at most an exhortation to be good citizens, but we were surprised.

Catherine fixed her eyes on us. "You have set goals for yourselves. I have heard some of them. But I don't think you have set them high enough. You have talent and intelligence and a chance. I think you should take those goals and expand them. Think of the most you could do with your lives. Make what you do matter. Above all, dream big."

It was not so much an instruction as a dare. I felt stunned, like a small animal fixed on bright lights. This woman I admired so much was disappointed in us—not by what we were but by how little we aspired to be.

I won the America's Junior Miss contest that year. In the fall I entered Wellesley College, where my sister, Linda, was beginning her junior year. I graduated in 1967 with a B.A. in English and a complete lack of inspiration about what I should do with it.

I went to my father, a lawyer and later a judge in Louisville's Jefferson County Court. "What is it that you enjoy doing most?" he asked.

"Writing," I replied slowly. "I like the power of the word. And working with people. And being in touch with what's happening in the world."

He thought for a moment. "Did you ever consider television?" I hadn't.

At that time there were few if any women journalists on television in our part of the country. The idea of being a pioneer in the field sounded like dreaming big. So that's how I came to get up my nerve, put on my very best Mary Tyler Moore girl journalist outfit, and go out to convince the news director at Louisville's WLKY-TV to let me have a chance.

He gave it to me. For the next two and a half years, I worked as a combination weather and news reporter.

Eventually, though, I began to feel restless. I'd lie awake at night feeling that something wasn't right. I'd wait for the revelation, the sign pointing in the direction of the Big Dream. What I didn't realize is what Catherine Marshall undoubtedly knew all along—that the dream is not the destination but the journey.

I was still working at WLKY when my father was killed in an auto crash. His death—coupled with my urge to make a change—spurred me in the search for a different job and also kindled my interest in the world of government, law, and politics. I racked my brain. I put out feelers. Then one of my father's associates said, "What about Washington?"

Several months later, I said good-bye to my mother and Linda and to the good folks at WLKY, and boarded a plane for Washington, DC.

Now, I know this may sound incredibly naive, but when the plane landed at National Airport, I got off with a very firm idea of where I wanted to work—at the White House. True, in the eyes of official Washington I might have been right off the equivalent of the turnip truck, but working in the White House was exactly what I had in mind!

Thanks to a few kind words of recommendation from a friend of my father's, I was able to obtain an interview with Ron Ziegler, the White House press secretary, and I was hired.

Those were heady days. The Press Office, located in the West Wing of the White House, was the hub for information flowing between the White House and the media. I worked hard and I worked long and loved every part of it.

Then came Watergate.

In the summer of 1974, the president resigned. Immediately I was appointed to his transition team in San Clemente, California.

My assignment on the West Coast was supposed to last only six months. But a few days after my arrival the president made a request that I was totally unprepared for. He asked me to consider staying on in San Clemente—along with several other writers and aides—to assist him in researching and writing his memoirs. I had to make a choice, and a choice that I knew would have consequences.

"Career suicide," mumbled some of my friends.

But I had worked for this man and he had been good to me. Now he was asking me for something that I was in a position to give. I stayed. I have never regretted the decision.

One day in the long exile from television, Catherine Marshall and her husband, Leonard LeSourd, called to say they were nearby. They came for a visit, and again I felt the searching gaze and, implicit in it, the words, "What is next?" Once more I came to appreciate the immense power of someone who is unafraid to hold other people to a standard. And again I realized the way a single uncompromising question can force reexamination of a life.

After three years as co-anchor on the CBS Morning News, I became co-editor of CBS's *60 Minutes* television newsmagazine. We worked at a breakneck pace with long hours and constant travel thrown in. I kept a suitcase packed at all times, so that I could be ready to fly out on assignment at a moment's notice.

My New York apartment, which I saw far too little of those days, became my refuge, the place where I was free to pad about in jeans and a sweatshirt—no makeup, no contact lenses, no hairspray. Sometimes I would unwind by playing the piano. Or I would relax by doing something simple but satisfying—baking a pan of muffins or cleaning out an old junk drawer. These were the times of silent reassessment.

No matter when I go out into the world again—and who knows where I'll be flying next?—I can almost hear a wonderful woman prodding me with her fiery challenge to stretch further and, no matter how big the dream, to dream a little bigger still. God, she seems to be saying, can forgive failure, but not failing to try.

Dreams and Prayers

*Do not pray for dreams
equal to your powers.
Pray for powers
equal to your dreams.*

ADELAIDE PROCTOR

The Child I Couldn't Have

BY ROSE SINCLAIR

Thank you for letting me know," I told the nurse on the phone. Then I hung up, fighting back tears.

The tests had just come back from the lab. They confirmed what I had feared all along—that my husband Jay and I would never be able to have children. Now, as I walked through our big house, its halls echoing with emptiness, I longed to fill them with the sounds of a child.

Then the guilt that I thought I was rid of came surging back. It stemmed from the fact that when I was nineteen, before I met and married Jay, I became pregnant. I gave the baby up for adoption. Even though giving him up was like giving up a part of myself, I knew I had no way to take care of him all by myself.

For months afterward I had terrible nightmares. I awoke at night sweating profusely, remembering the squalling of that tiny, wrinkled, red infant just after birth. I heaped the guilt upon myself, not realizing that if I had just asked for it, God's love would have enfolded me.

That evening I gave Jay the sad news when he got home. I told him I was sure that God was punishing me for the mistake I had made as a teenager.

"Don't feel that way, Rose," Jay said, trying to comfort me. "I'm sure He knows what He's doing."

I buried my face in the warm hollow of Jay's shoulder.

We began to consider adoption, but I viewed it as a very distant hope. I really wasn't seeing God as a working force in my life, despite my professed belief. The truth was, I wouldn't let Him be.

"There aren't many infants available," the doctor told us. "Would you consider adopting an older child?"

"I want an infant so badly!" I felt my feverish longing nearly burst through to the surface. *I want someone to replace my own little boy*, I thought to myself.

"I know. I understand," the doctor said. "It may take awhile, but we can try to find a baby for you," he assured us, recommending that we contact an adoption agency to begin the process of interviews and forms and home visits as soon as possible—which we did.

Months went by without hearing anything further from the adoption agency after the initial application process and home study. In the meantime I immersed myself in gardening. I spent the warmer spring days preparing the ground for seed and planting. In six weeks' time I was rewarded by a rosy rim of radishes pushing through the dark soil and the tender arched heads of little beanstalks proudly growing in line.

I watched them grow into tall, healthy plants, and I found I had a kind of maternal feeling toward them.

Finally the adoption agency called. "We have a five-year-old boy who is available for adoption."

I was filled with bitterness. "I told you I wanted a baby, not a full-grown child," I said, trying to keep my voice even.

"Yes, I know. But we try to give you the opportunity to consider older children when they become available."

"Thank you." I slammed down the phone and, tears streaming down my cheeks, ran outside.

Stumbling, I ran between the rows of beans and corn in my garden and finally slumped down in the trench that I had dug for the water drainage. When my self-pitying tears finally abated, I looked around me at the garden I had "mothered" all spring. There next to me was the first fruit of my labor, a small cluster of green beans hidden in the intertwining leaves of a beanstalk. I longed to be able to nurture a small human being the way I had those beans.

Suddenly, as I sat there, the only answer became as clear as if God were speaking to me. Had I ever asked God to forgive me for what I had done so many years before? Or had I assumed that my sin was too great for Him to forgive?

"Oh, God, forgive me," I croaked.

My thoughts tumbled and rolled. A part of me seemed to be lifted out, as if it were a burden I never really knew I was carrying. I felt God's presence caress me as I sat there among the leaves of the beanstalks in the golden gleam of the corn silks with the sweet, strong smell of the earth all around me. My son would be five now, I suddenly realized—the same age as the boy the agency had called me about. Why hadn't that occurred to me before?

Momentarily I shoved the thought aside. *Someone will want him*, I thought as I headed toward the house. But inside I knew that children over three were often extremely hard to place, and that that little boy needed a home, needed us, now.

Moments later, as if in a dream, I found myself dialing Jay's office number.

"Jay? Listen, the people from the adoption agency called today...." As I had known, it didn't matter to Jay how old the child was.

As I dialed the agency's number, I could feel more warm tears coursing down my cheeks. "Could you tell me if you've placed that little five-year-old boy yet?" I asked the social worker. "I think we'd like to meet him."

When Jay and I arrived at the adoption agency, I saw the inscription over the doorway once again, and this time I understood its real meaning for me: YOUR CHILDREN ARE NOT YOUR OWN, BUT THEY BELONG TO YOUR FATHER WHO IS IN HEAVEN.

While we waited to meet our future son, those words made me realize that it didn't really matter who was the parent and who was the child. We are all God's children. I understood that so clearly when we met Brian—a slender, blond little guy with a wide grin that revealed a missing front tooth, a child anxious for love and affection and the security we could give him.

Of course, from that day on, it was not all easy. There were barriers we had to break down in order to get to know one another, to fit into each other's patterns.

But the greatest reward has been that since then I have felt the comforting presence of God so many times, often in the simple laughter that fills our house now, but mostly in the precious gift of love that Brian has given to us.

My life would surely be different if I hadn't uttered those four simple words asking for God's forgiveness that day in my vegetable garden. I am so thankful that God filled me with His Spirit—changing me and making me able to be open and loving to the child He had waiting for us.

Better Plans

God specializes in things fresh and firsthand.
His plans for you this year may outshine those
of the past.... He's preparing to fill your days
with reasons to give Him praise.

JONI EARECKSON TADA

A Note from the Editors

Guideposts, a nonprofit organization, touches millions of lives every day through products and services that inspire, encourage, and uplift. Our magazines, books, prayer network, and outreach programs help people connect their faith-filled values to their daily lives. To learn more, visit Guideposts.org or GuidepostsFoundation.org.